YORK NOTES

2

TESS OF THE D'URBERVILLES

THOMAS HARDY

NOTES BY KAREN SAYER

 Longman

York Press

The right of Karen Sayer to be identified as Author
of this Work has been asserted by her in accordance with the
Copyright, Designs and Patents Act 1988

YORK PRESS
322 Old Brompton Road, London SW5 9JH

PEARSON EDUCATION LIMITED
Edinburgh Gate, Harlow,
Essex CM20 2JE, United Kingdom
Associated companies, branches and representatives throughout the world

First published 1998
This new and fully revised edition first published 2005

10 9 8 7 6 5 4 3 2 1

ISBN 1–405–80707–5

Typeset by Land & Unwin (Data Sciences), Bugbrooke, Northamptonshire
Produced by Pearson Education Asia Limited, Hong Kong

CONTENTS

PART FOUR
CRITICAL HISTORY

PART FIVE
BACKGROUND

PART ONE

INTRODUCTION

HOW TO STUDY A NOVEL

Studying a novel on your own requires self-discipline and a carefully thought-out work plan in order to be effective.

- You will need to read the novel more than once. Start by reading it quickly for pleasure, then read it slowly and thoroughly.

- On your second reading make detailed notes on the plot, characters and themes of the novel. Further readings will generate new ideas and help you to memorise the details of the story.

- Some of the characters will develop as the plot unfolds. How do your responses towards them change during the course of the novel?

- Think about how the novel is narrated. From whose point of view are events described?

- A novel may or may not present events chronologically: the time-scheme may be a key to its structure and organisation.

- What part do the settings play in the novel?

- Are words, images or incidents repeated so as to give the work a pattern? Do such patterns help you to understand the novel's themes?

- Identify what styles of language are used in the novel.

- What is the effect of the novel's ending? Is the action completed and closed, or left incomplete and open?

- Does the novel present a moral and just world?

- Cite exact sources for all quotations, whether from the text itself or from critical commentaries. Wherever possible find your own examples from the novel to back up your opinions.

- Always express your ideas in your own words.

These York Notes offer an introduction to *Tess of the d'Urbervilles* and cannot substitute for close reading of the text and the study of secondary sources.

CHECK THE FILM

The first film adaptation of *Tess of the d'Urbervilles* was made for Metro-Goldwyn Pictures Corporation in 1924. Now presumed lost, it was a silent movie directed by Marshall Neilan and starring Blanche Sweet and Conrad Nagel.

READING *TESS OF THE D'URBERVILLES*

Hardy's novels are generally pessimistic and *Tess of the d'Urbervilles* is no exception. As we read *Tess* we come to fear the unfolding of an almost brutal plot. The reader is tormented by shades of alternative worlds in which Tess and Angel, even Alec, might live happily ever after, and a sense of the malign lingers long after the novel has been finished. But Hardy also celebrates plenitude, deals in desire and writes of small, ordinary moments of cheerfulness:

CHECK THE FILM
Roman Polanski's adaptation, *Tess* (1979), filmed over eight months across forty locations in France, won three Oscars in 1981: Best Cinematography, Best Costume Design and Best Art Direction.

Mrs Durbeyfield was balanced on one foot beside the tub, the other ... rocking her youngest child ... Nick-knock, nick-knock, went the cradle; the candle-flame stretched itself tall, and began jigging up and down; the water dribbled from the matron's elbows, and the song galloped on to the end of the verse ... Even now ... Joan Durbeyfield was a passionate lover of tune. (Chapter 3, pp. 57–8)

It is easy to become fascinated by the extraordinary texture of Hardy's writing. Some critics have characterised his style as 'bad', because he uses very complex phrasing and seems to make up words. However, Hardy uses his odd language to create a feeling of involvement which, in turn, helps us to see what is essentially mundane in a new light. Hardy, for instance, teaches us to see Tess Durbeyfield as a woman whose beauty is enhanced by her little imperfections.

Hardy initially found it very hard to get his novel published and finally had to employ self-censorship before any of the weekly journals would take it as a serial. This was because the novel, for the Victorians, was morally sensitive. The central character is of course described in the subtitle as 'pure', but she has an illegitimate child, becomes involved in an adulterous relationship and is a murderess.

Many critics have treated Tess like a real person and asked, as the Duchess of Abercorn did at the time of publication, 'Do you support her or not?' The debate over whether Tess was raped or seduced, whether she is a total or partial victim, a justified or blameworthy murderess, still rages. But Tess is a complex character who cannot be pinned down. She is both a victim and a murderess and this is what makes *Tess* so bewitching.

CHECK THE FILM
One of the most recent adaptations was directed by Ian Sharp in 1998 for the BBC. This version claims to remain closer to the original text than Roman Polanski's 1979 adaptation, *Tess*, but has not received the same critical acclaim.

PART TWO

THE TEXT

NOTE ON THE TEXT

Originally contracted for serialisation by Tillotson and Son, but turned down on moral grounds in its early stages, *Tess of the d'Urbervilles* was initially written in book form. Later, the novel was edited by Hardy in order to get it published as a serial. This was largely due to financial need and the novel was simply divided into five books to facilitate serialisation, but these books do not correspond with the seven phases of the novel. Hardy realised the necessity of reworking the content of the text for the serials market when it was further rejected by *Murray's Magazine* and by *Macmillan's Magazine*, again due to its treatment of seduction and illegitimate birth. *Tess* therefore finally came out as a weekly serial in the *Graphic* from 4 July to 26 December 1891 – it was published simultaneously in *Harper's Bazaar* in the United States. The editing included the removal of all references to Tess's seduction and to her child, while Angel Clare had to carry the milkmaids across the flood by wheelbarrow, rather than in his arms. The missing elements were then reworked for publication as short sketches. The baptism of Tess's child came out as 'The Midnight Baptism. A Study of Christianity' in the *Fortnightly Review*, May 1891; the seduction scene as 'Saturday Night in Arcady' in the Literary Supplement of the Edinburgh *National Observer*, 14 November 1891.

The edited, serialised version was published as a book after serialisation, but it took some time and several editions before the text finally came together in its complete form. This was because Hardy continued to work steadily on the novel, writing and rewriting it. The first, serialised edition therefore came out in 1891, but *Tess* was not really stable as a text until the 1912 'definitive' Macmillan *Wessex Novels* edition was published. It is this later edition that is now usually reprinted as the final text, though Hardy continued to make minor changes after this date. Of the contemporary reprints, that published in Penguin Classics, 1978,

CHECK THE BOOK

J. A. Sutherland's *Victorian Novelists and Publishers* (Athlone Press, 1976) still provides a good summary of Hardy's publication history and relationship with his publisher.

CONTEXT

Periodical publication expanded rapidly during the nineteenth century and it is probable that the readership for periodicals exceeded that for books. The periodical press was therefore hugely influential.

is probably the most useful, as it not only includes an invaluable introduction by A. Alvarez, but also textual notes by David Skilton, which cover and comment on the key differences between the 1891 and 1912 editions and the author's several prefaces.

SYNOPSIS

The novel, as the title suggests, is about a young woman called Tess Durbeyfield. It is structured around seven phases which reflect the pattern of her short life. In the first phase, The Maiden, Tess's father finds out about his ancestors – the d'Urbervilles – and gets so drunk in celebration of this, even though 'There are several families among the cottagers … of almost equal lustre', according to the parson (Chapter 1, p. 45), that he cannot drive to market. Tess goes instead, and the family's horse dies in a terrible accident. The remorseful Tess, under encouragement from her mother and father, goes to a Mrs d'Urberville to seek help. Mrs d'Urberville, however, is not really, as they all suppose, a distant relative. The surname has simply been assumed by a successful commercial family who have recently moved to the area. While on her errand, Tess meets Mrs d'Urberville's son Alec, who finally arranges for Tess to be employed on his mother's estate. While Tess is there, Alec keeps seeking her out and eventually dishonours her.

In the second phase, Maiden No More, Tess, now pregnant, returns home from Trantridge. Guilt-ridden and ashamed, only venturing out at dusk, Tess hides in her family's cottage. Once she has had her illegitimate child, Sorrow, she goes back to work and finds that she is generally accepted by her community. The child, however, dies and though she hopes to save his soul by carrying out her own christening, he is still buried in an unmarked grave. Tess stays in the village for a while, but eventually feels that it would be better to start afresh somewhere new.

In the third phase, The Rally, Tess leaves home again and this time takes work for the spring and summer on a dairy farm far away from everyone she knows. While working at Talbothays she meets Angel Clare – he actually first appears, very briefly, at the beginning

 CHECK THE NET
You can find a reliable e-text of *Tess of the d'Urbervilles,* at **http://www. online-literature. com**

**www. CHECK
THE NET**
The novel is set in
Hardy's fictional
county Wessex.
The Thomas Hardy
Association
website includes a
reproduction of
Hardy's own map
of Tess's country:
search **http://www.
yale.edu**

of the book – a clergyman's son. He is working at the dairy in order to learn something about farming. He would have gone to university like his brothers, but for the fact that he has rejected his family's very rigid Christianity.

Tess and Clare begin to fall in love and this is very hard for Tess, who cannot quite bring herself to tell Clare about Alec and Sorrow, though she knows that she should do so. The tension builds as Tess and Clare move towards marriage in the fourth phase, The Consequence. She tries to write a letter to Angel, in which she confesses everything, but he never receives it and the fourth phase ends on their wedding night, as Clare confesses his own youthful misdemeanours.

As we enter the fifth phase, The Woman Pays, Tess finally tells all. Unable to see the parallels between their previous experiences, Clare shuns her and declares that she is no longer the woman he loved: 'You were one person; now you are another' (Chapter 35, p. 298). Tess goes home and Angel emigrates to Brazil. He has left her money to take care of herself, but after helping her parents repair their house – they are deceived by Tess into believing in a reconciliation, and therefore have high expectations of her new-found wealth – she is left with very little to live on and must find a job for the winter. She ends up working at Flintcomb-Ash, where the work is particularly hard. Her old friends from the dairy farm are there and they eventually persuade her to seek help from Angel's family – the Clare family are also oblivious to the failure of the marriage. However, she overhears Angel's brothers and his old fiancée talking disparagingly about the marriage, so she moves on quickly without seeking his parents' aid. While walking back, she is surprised to see Alec, recently converted, preaching in a barn.

In the sixth phase, The Convert, Alec's faith is tried by Tess. He becomes newly fascinated by her and offers to marry her, but when she tells him that she cannot, he persists in pursuing her. Alec loses his faith, but still offers to help her and her family. For a while Tess manages to fend him off, but when she suddenly has to return home to look after her mother and her father, she begins to weaken. Soon after this, Tess's father dies and her family are forced to leave their cottage. Again, Alec appears and offers help, and, as the family's new arrangements fall through, her determination to have nothing more to do with him begins to crumble.

In the seventh and final phase, Fulfilment, Angel returns from Brazil. Thanks to his experiences abroad, he has changed. He eventually tracks Tess and Alec down to a lodging house in Sandbourne. He seeks reconciliation, but, seeing that she is well provided for, quickly leaves. Tess goes back to her rooms in distress and, furious that Alec had lied to her about Angel ever coming back to her, she murders him. She runs after Angel. They manage to outwit their pursuers and are blissfully happy for a week. They are finally tracked down at Stonehenge where Tess makes Angel promise that he will care for her younger sister 'Liza-Lu. Tess is arrested and, in the final chapter, hanged, watched from afar by 'two speechless gazers bent … down to the earth, as if in prayer' (Chapter 59, pp. 489–90).

DETAILED SUMMARIES

PHASE THE FIRST – THE MAIDEN

CHAPTER 1

- Parson Tringham tells Jack Durbeyfield that he is a d'Urberville.

While walking home from market one May evening Jack Durbeyfield meets Parson Tringham. Jack wants to know why the parson has been calling him 'Sir John' lately. The parson tells him that he is descended from 'the ancient and knightly family of the d'Urbervilles' (p. 43), a family that is now 'extinct in the male line' and that he should reflect on '"how are the mighty fallen"' (p. 45). Jack, already slightly drunk, decides to celebrate. He sends a boy for a carriage from The Pure Drop Inn, complete with a noggin of rum on account. He gives the boy a shilling, asks him to tell his wife to stop washing and for them 'at hwome' (p. 47) to cook him a fine

CONTEXT

Pagan was a relatively rare Norman-French name, related to Payn, but as a word carries a number of useful connotations for Hardy, including reference not only to heathen and non-Christian practices and beliefs, but also, via *paganus* and *pagus*, to rusticity and the countryside. The French *pagus*, in particular, refers to a landmark fixed in the earth.

CHAPTER 1 continued

CONTEXT

Hardy derived the fictional name d'Urberville from the real name Turberville. The Turbervilles were lords of the manor during the thirteenth century in Bere Regis, Dorset (Hardy's Kingsbere). Durbeyfield is also close to the related Turberville derivative Turbyfield. The Turberville name also occurs with reference to King William I's creation of marcher lordships, each of which had near royal prerogatives. Among these was the marcher lord Robert FitzHamon, Lord of Glamorgan, whose retinue included one Sir Payn de Turberville (nicknamed 'the Demon'). Though not given land by FitzHamon, de Turberville nonetheless acquired it by taking over the lordship of Coity Castle, Wales.

dinner. Just as the boy sets out a brass band can be heard in the distance; it is the 'women's club-walking' (p. 47) in which, the boy reminds Jack, his daughter is participating.

COMMENTARY

Detailed description and dialect generate a feeling that Hardy is telling the reader a real story about real people, a sense of verisimilitude. Class and social mobility come to the fore in the relationship between Jack and the parson. There is extensive use of historical and geographical detail – in the first sentence we find reference to 'the adjoining Vale of Blakemore or Blackmoor' (p. 43) – the peasantry are linked both to the locality and to the broader historical process, the history of England.

This opening chapter introduces the issue of Tess's ancestry and later on Tess will visit the tombs of her forebears, as described to Jack. Many future events are hinted at in the chapter and this extensive use of foreshadowing is typical of the earlier phases of the novel. The family's ongoing decline seems inevitable and Tess's fate seems sealed. Jack is already drunk, on top of which he immediately starts racking up debts and giving away money. Jack is proud like his ancestors, and we will see the same characteristic emerge in Tess. The inevitability of loss and suffering becomes a key theme in the novel.

GLOSSARY

43	haggler travelling dealer
44	Battle Abbey Roll the records kept at Battle Abbey – the abbey founded where the Battle of Hastings (1066) took place – which list those who came over with William the Conqueror
	Pipe Rolls early exchequer records of annual county accounts
	King Stephen reigned 1135–54
	King John reigned 1199–1216
	Edward the Second reigned 1307–27
	Oliver Cromwell Lord Protector 1649–58
	Charles the Second reigned 1660–85
45	wold (dialect) old
	'how are the mighty fallen' Bible, II Samuel 1:19, 25
47	skillentons (dialect) skeletons

47	lamb's fry lamb's testicles
	black-pot black pudding, sausage made from pig's blood
	chitterlings pig's intestines (fry, black-pot and chitterlings were all eaten by the poor)
	club-walking annual mutual benefit society holiday
	vamp (dialect) to tramp

CHAPTER 2

- Tess Durbeyfield is spurned by Angel Clare at the village club-walking.

The village women are celebrating the coming of spring. While the women, dressed all in white, process around the parish, Jack Durbeyfield is driven home in a cart. Comment is passed, much to the embarrassment of one young member of the group: Tess Durbeyfield. The discomfiture forgotten, Tess and the other women reach the end of their promenade and begin dancing. They are watched by three young gentlemen, one of whom, Angel, decides to join in. Angel does not dance with Tess, but, reflecting on the scene from afar, he reproaches himself for missing the opportunity.

COMMENTARY

We meet Tess for the first time in this chapter. Again future events in the novel are foreshadowed. Description is predominant. Tess, for instance, who is 'a fine and handsome girl … [with a] mobile peony mouth and large innocent eyes … wore a red ribbon in her hair, and was the only one of the white company who could boast of such a pronounced adornment' (p. 51). Here we see Tess as an innocent country maid, but the complexities of her character that, in part, give rise to her later misfortunes begin to become apparent. The issue of class returns with more force in the three brothers, two of whom scorn dancing with working-class girls. Tess seems to be part of the landscape, in contrast to Angel, who is like a tourist and

> **CONTEXT**
>
> Angel was a name suggested to Hardy by a memorial in Stinsford parish church. The most popular given first names in the UK in 1880 were Mary and William.

CHECK THE BOOK

For an extended discussion of the meanings attached to the use of the colour red in *Tess*, and especially images of red on white, see Tony Tanner, 'Colour and Movement in Hardy's *Tess of the d'Urbervilles*', in Ian Watt, ed., *The Victorian Novel: Modern Essays in Criticism* (Oxford University Press, 1971).

moves through it very quickly. The issue of the period in which the text is set is raised here – possibly after 1860 if *A Counterblast to Agnosticism* is read as 'A Counterblast to Essays [and] Reviews'.

GLOSSARY

48	plashed interwoven
49	King Henry III 1216–72
	Cerealia celebrations for Ceres, Roman goddess of agriculture
	Old Style the calendar was changed in 1752 and called the New Style
50	'I have no pleasure in them' Bible, Ecclesiastes 12:1
51	market-nitch (dialect) the amount drunk at market
52	uncribbed, uncabined Shakespeare, *Macbeth*, Act III Scene 4, 'cabin'd, cribb'd, confin'd', i.e. free and unconstrained
53	hoyden contemptuous term for a young girl
	A Counterblast to Agnosticism fictional title, but typical of Victorian religious rhetoric
	clipsing and colling (dialect) embracing and hugging

CHAPTER 3

- Joan Durbeyfield joins Jack in celebrating their good fortune.

Tess returns home to find her mother singing, rocking the youngest child in its cradle and still engaged in her housework. Jack, having told his wife about their good fortune, as he sees it, has gone to the pub, Rolliver's. Joan Durbeyfield fills Tess in on the good news. She also tells Tess that Jack's health is failing, then goes to 'fetch' him, as he is to set out on a delivery in the early hours. Tess is left to look after her brothers and sisters until, tired of waiting, she sends her little brother Abraham after them. When he fails to return she goes to get them back herself.

COMMENTARY

Here we are introduced to the rest of the Durbeyfields. Again, there is extensive use of foreshadowing. The divisions within Tess's character that we were introduced to in the last chapter are added to. Tess, we are told, 'spoke two languages; the dialect at home, more or less; ordinary English abroad and to persons of quality' (p. 58). She is both educated yet remains a peasant. The descriptions of Joan, the children and the cottage reflect Tess's odd mixture of sympathy and contempt for her family. Here we begin to understand slightly more of Tess as we see her dreary home and as we are introduced to her rather bawdy mother – who would never have been able to understand the narrator's comment that she drank because then her problems took on 'a metaphysical impalpability' (p. 60).

GLOSSARY

56	**gallopade** lively dance-tune
57	**diment** diamond
	Cubit's i.e. Cupid's, Roman god of love
58	**fess** (dialect) lively, brisk; conceited, proud
	Sixth Standard in the National School the highest level attainable in the schools run by the National Society for Promoting the Education of the Poor in the Principles of the Established Church, founded in 1811
	mommet (dialect) scarecrow
	thik that
	larry (dialect) confusion or commotion
59	**Oliver Grumble** Oliver Cromwell
	Saint Charles means Charles II, who was far from saintly
	plim (dialect) swell
	vlee (dialect) a fly, i.e. one-horse carriage hired out
	mampus (dialect) crowd
61	**Revised Code** annual codes were issued by the Education Department setting out conditions for obtaining grants. The National Schools were funded in part by government

continued

CONTEXT

National schools existed throughout the country and were one of the main ways in which the poor could have access to education until the 1870 Education Act, which made education available to all; and the 1891 Education Act, which made education free.

grants and used the monitorial system in order to run cheaply – this used older pupils to teach younger pupils, so that only one teacher was needed for up to five hundred children. The Revised Code (1862) tied the size of the grant to the number of pupils and their results in standard exams in an attempt by the state to reduce costs.

61   Jacobean time of James I, who reigned 1603–25

62   'Nature's holy plan' William Wordsworth, 'Lines Written in Early Spring', line 22

CHAPTER 4

- Joan and Jack start thinking about how to make the most of their family connections.
- Prince is killed.

CHECK THE BOOK

To find out more about animals in nineteenth-century English thought, see Harriet Ritvo, *The Animal Estate: The English and Other Creatures in Victorian England* (Penguin, 1990).

Joan joins her husband at Rolliver's. She remembers that there is a rich woman living in Trantridge called d'Urberville. Assuming that this lady is a relative, she considers sending Tess over 'to claim kin' (p. 65). Abraham enters, but cannot get them to leave. The speculations as to what may come of claiming kin continue until Tess arrives. When the time comes for Jack to go to Casterbridge market, he cannot get up. Tess offers to go if Abraham will accompany her. They drive through the night talking about fate, but they doze off and, as their wagon drifts to the far side of the road, the morning mail-cart ploughs into them. Their horse, Prince, bleeds to death.

COMMENTARY

This chapter initially shifts back in time to the middle of Chapter 3. The Durbeyfield family, aside from Tess, are clearly shown to be shiftless and idle, but ambitious. They may not have a good grasp of history, or even the moral dangers they are exposing Tess to –

recognised by some of the other drinkers as getting 'green malt in floor' (p. 66) – but they are sensitive to economic need.

The chapter is loaded with foreboding. Tess seems doomed; the blood splashing on her, red on white, is particularly ominous. Seeing herself as a 'murderess' (p. 73), she will eventually commit murder.

GLOSSARY

63	**it was better to drink … in a wide house** Bible, Proverbs 21:9: 'It is better to dwell in a corner of the housetop, than with a brawling woman in a wide house'
	cwoffer (dialect) coffer, chest
64	**Solomon's temple** Bible, I Kings 7:15–22
65	**sumple** (dialect) supple, pliant
66	**fine figure o' fun** (colloquial) good-looking
	get green malt in floor (colloquial) become pregnant
	eastings (colloquial) turning to the east during church service
67	**nater** (dialect) nature
69	**stubbard-tree** early apple tree

CHAPTER 5

- Tess is persuaded to seek help for her family.
- She catches Alec d'Urberville's eye.

Because Tess blames herself for the catastrophe and the consequent decline in her family's fortunes, she agrees to visit Mrs d'Urberville. However, the d'Urbervilles who live at The Slopes are not relatives, they have simply adopted the name 'd'Urberville' to disguise their commercial origins.

Tess is met by Mrs d'Urberville's son, Alec. When Tess explains her errand, he calls her 'my pretty Coz' (p. 80) and shows her around.

CONTEXT

It was commonplace in the nineteenth century for antiquarians like Parson Tringham to study aristocratic lineages. It was also commonplace for 'new money' to buy into the status and authority of an aristocratic name.

He gives her some strawberries and makes her eat one from his hand. He gives her roses and gets her to place some in her bosom. After lunch he promises that he will try to help.

COMMENTARY

Hardy uses an **omniscient narrator** here. This provides us with information that Tess does not have access to, to signal the significant part that Alec will play in her destiny, and to provide us with some of the philosophical framework of the novel. Alec looks like a villain. The fact that The Slopes is a decorative hobby farm, built purely for pleasure, so that '[e]verything looked like money – like the last coin issued from the Mint' (p. 77), acts as an omen. The primitive associations of The Chase contrast with Tess's stammering innocence. Nevertheless, Tess is sensitive to the fact that the d'Urbervilles may not be all that they seem, and we learn about her character here, especially through the short flashback to her childhood.

CHECK THE BOOK

In his *Essay on the Principle of Population* (1798) Malthus proposed that the population would naturally grow faster than humanity's ability to feed itself, and discussed natural and artificial ways in which population growth might be checked.

GLOSSARY		
74	good-now (dialect) equivalent to 'you must know', 'I guess' or 'you know'	
76	Malthusian someone who follows T. R. Malthus (1766–1834)	
77	Druidical mistletoe mistletoe was held to be sacred by the pre-Christian Druids	
	sylvan wooded, rustic setting	
	Chapels-of-Ease chapels built to serve remote areas	
80	Coz a colloquial familiarity, short for cousin	
83	crumby (slang) appealing	

CHAPTER 6

- Tess is asked to go and work on the d'Urberville estate.

Tess travels home, decked out in flowers. Of all the omens she encounters that day, the only one she notices is 'a thorn of the rose remaining in her breast [that] accidentally [pricks] her chin' (p. 84). Joan is enthusiastic when Tess is offered work on Mrs d'Urberville's poultry farm, but Tess is reluctant to take it. In the end Alec himself turns up and Joan becomes convinced that he will marry Tess. Tess is flattered but still resists until the children start nagging and teasing her. She had hoped to become a teacher, but in the light of the horse's death sets this ambition aside to help her family.

COMMENTARY

The desire to help her family prompts Tess to act selflessly, against her better judgement. This thematic pattern is repeated when Alec tries to persuade Tess to take up with him again after Clare has left her. Tess is expected to trade her womanliness, and not just her labour, to help her family.

> **GLOSSARY**
>
> 87   dolorifuge (neologism) chases away sorrow
> 88   fairlings (dialect) presents; things bought at a fair
>   spring-cart cart with spring suspension

CHAPTER 7

- Tess leaves home decked out in her finest and is picked up by Alec.

Tess puts on some plain work clothes, but her mother washes her hair and dresses her up in her club-walking best. Jack says he will sell the name and speculates about the price he should ask for it. Tess is finally seen off by her mother and siblings. Just as she is about to get into the spring-cart, Alec appears. Joan is delighted. Tess shows some reluctance to get into his gig, but eventually sits beside him and is whisked away. That night Joan wishes she had made further enquiries about the young man's character; still, she assures herself, 'if he don't marry her afore he will after' (p. 93).

> **CONTEXT**
>
> In the nineteenth century working-class women's 'respectability' depended in part on the type of paid employment they took. At this point, working with poultry and young farm animals was seen to be quite appropriate for girls and women.

 CHECK THE BOOK

For a detailed analysis of the way in which Tess, like all Victorian women, must trade on her femininity, read John Goode, 'Woman and the Literary Text' in Juliet Mitchell and Ann Oakley, eds., *The Rights and Wrongs of Women* (Penguin, 1976). Also see Goode's *Thomas Hardy, The Offensive Truth* (Blackwell, 1988).

CONTEXT

It was relatively common practice among the rural working class, much to the horror of urban middle-class reformers, to marry only once a baby was on the way.

COMMENTARY

The Durbeyfields are not as naive as they might seem. Jack is well aware of the financial possibilities of trading in names. Joan, while she seems to bank on Tess's marketability, still recognises the dangers her daughter will face. Tess seems to seal her own fate by giving herself up both to Alec and to her mother's artful ministrations. When Tess leaves the cottage she is not herself, but an idealised image of herself, and this is a key theme in the book. Tess always rises to the occasion as the exception to the rule, and many of her troubles arise from the fact that men like Alec misread and idealise her. Her departure is described at a distance which dramatises her final moment of decision.

GLOSSARY

89	**dand** (dialect) dandy
91	**lammicken** (dialect) clumsy, slouching
92	**gig** light, two-wheeled open carriage
	dog-cart open carriage with crosswise back-to-back seats
	buck smart young man, dandy
93	**choice over her** (colloquial) attracted by her

CHAPTER 8

- Alec frightens Tess with his reckless driving.
- He demands a kiss before he will slow down.

Alec drives off with Tess, who quickly becomes alarmed at his recklessness. He says that he will drive more carefully if she will let him kiss her cheek. She agrees, but dodges him and, though 'd'Urberville gave her the kiss of mastery' (p. 96), she then wipes the kiss off. Before the next downward slope begins she loses her hat and once out of the cart refuses to get back in. They exchange harsh words, but finally Alec's temper cools and they walk on, Tess still on the ground, Alec in the gig.

COMMENTARY

Alec's intentions are made clear here; we also learn that he is reckless, cruel and violent. The speed of the gig is indicated more by description than by the use of short words or phrasing. There are parallels between Alec's mastery of the horse and his determination to master Tess. Tess is trapped by social convention, Alec's understanding of her morality as based on her class, her obligations to her family and, apparently, fate.

As she crosses from the vale to Trantridge, Tess moves **metaphorically** from childhood to womanhood. This is the point at which Tess also becomes an itinerant character within the novel, always on the move. Such characters are common within Hardy's work.

GLOSSARY

96	holmberry holly-berry – bright red

CHAPTER 9

- Tess starts working for the blind Mrs d'Urberville.

Tess starts work at The Slopes. The poultry, which are ornamental and treated like pets, live in an old cottage and Tess must take them up to her blind mistress for daily inspection. Alec teaches Tess how to whistle for the bullfinches in Mrs d'Urberville's bedroom. Slowly, he gets Tess to accept him. 'A familiarity with Alec d'Urberville's presence – which that young man carefully cultivated in her ... – removed much of her original shyness of him' (p. 103).

COMMENTARY

Again, we are told more than Tess knows. The issue of class is highlighted by the narrator's comments about the cottage in which the fowl are kept and the fact that Tess becomes 'more pliable under

CONTEXT

The image of the caged bird, and its association with Woman's position, became almost emblematic in nineteenth-century literature and art. For example, see Elizabeth Barrett Browning's poem *Aurora Leigh* (1857).

CONTEXT

Copyholders held land on an estate, based on conditions set down in a copy of the manorial roll. Their tenure could last a specified number of generations.

[Alec's] hands than a mere companionship would have made her' (p. 104), because she is dependent upon Mrs d'Urberville and therefore, ultimately, upon Alec himself. The way in which the old inhabitants were removed from this cottage echoes the way in which Tess's family will be removed from theirs in Chapter 51. Tess is trapped, like a caged bird, as Alec whistles to her. The chapter ends with a sense of suspense, with Tess being stalked by Alec or perhaps fate.

GLOSSARY

101	**Confirmation** ceremony at which children become full members of the Christian Church, by the laying-on of hands by a bishop
102	**sitting like *Im*-patience on a monument** adapted from 'She sat like Patience on a monument, / Smiling at grief', Shakespeare, *Twelfth Night*, Act II Scene 4
103	**'Take, O take those lips away'** first line of a song from Shakespeare, *Measure for Measure*, Act IV Scene 1
	out of her books (colloquial) out of favour
104	**freak** whim

CHAPTER 10

- On returning from her weekly outing to Chaseborough, Tess is caught up in an argument with her drunken co-workers.
- Alec rescues her.

Tess goes to a fair in Chaseborough. Because she does not want to go back alone, she has to stay very late at a dance. Alec offers her a lift home, but she declines. Finally, she and her inebriated companions set out into the misty moonlit night. As they walk Car Darch, the Queen of Spades – an old favourite of Alec's – finds that a jar of treacle has been spilling down her back. They all laugh at her and she begins to pick on Tess. The row escalates and Tess decides to get away just as Alec appears. Tess impulsively jumps up behind him and is whisked away.

COMMENTARY

Chapter 10 was left out of the *Graphic* edition. We are introduced to two incidental characters here – the Queen of Spades and the Queen of Diamonds – who reappear in Chapter 43. There are also parallels with Chapter 4; in both cases drunkenness allows the rural working class to feel somewhat more elevated and content than usual. Tess is clearly not like the others, though, as she rises above their earthy pleasures.

Notice the extensive reference to myth in the dance scene. Dance is often symbolic of the success or failure of a community for Hardy. This shows how Hardy is not intending to achieve a completely **naturalist** evocation of English peasant life. As we move from **realist** commentary into an otherworldly description of folk dance, we find that Tess's future is **ironically** prefigured in references to classical figures who have escaped pursuit. Alec's sudden appearance and 'red coal of a cigar' (p. 109) prefigures his devilish entry in Chapter 50.

CHECK THE BOOK

For a discussion of the relationship between dance and constructions of community in Hardy's writing, see Simon Gatrell, *Thomas Hardy and the Proper Study of Mankind* (Macmillan, 1993).

GLOSSARY

105	parish relief money for the poor
107	Pans ... Syrinxes Pan, Greek god of shepherds and huntsmen, pursued Syrinx, a water nymph, until she threw herself into a river and was turned into a reed
	Lotis ... Priapus Priapus, Greek god of fertility, pursued Lotis, daughter of the sea god, who turned into a lotus flower
	Sileni plural of Silenus, drunken companion of Bacchus, Roman god of wine
	jints (dialect) joints
108	nimbus halo
112	Praxitelean of Praxiteles, Greek sculptor, fourth century BC

CHAPTER 11

? QUESTION

Examine the theme of power and desire in *Tess of the d'Urbervilles* with particular reference to the relationship between Tess and Alec.

- Alec takes Tess into The Chase.
- Is she raped?

Alec rides away from the villagers. As they slow to a walk the fog thickens, and Alec presses Tess to treat him like a lover. Tess is tired but realises that they have not been travelling towards Trantridge as she expected. Alec says that they are in The Chase, but he is unclear about their location and offers to leave her with his horse while he finds out where they are. On his return he finds her asleep on some leaves and bends down to feel her breath on his face, his cheek next to hers and the tears on her lashes. And, an 'immeasurable social chasm was to divide our heroine's personality thereafter from that previous self of hers who stepped from her mother's door to try her fortune at Trantridge poultry-farm' (p. 119).

COMMENTARY

Most of this chapter was missing from the *Graphic*. The sexual implications of the scene meant that it had to be censored, and even now what actually happens between Tess and Alec remains unclear. The fog and mist – symbols that are used repeatedly in the novel – work **metaphorically**, like the references to the primeval wood, to suggest sexual impropriety. The references to Tess's ancestors add to this and contribute to the pervasive sense of fatalism. The chapter is tense and drawn out, due to the contrast between Tess and Alec's dialogue, the descriptions of the rising fog, the slow movement of the horse, and the stillness of the final scene.

GLOSSARY

119   the ironical Tishbite   Elijah. When the priests of Baal fail to get a response from their god, he says 'either he is talking, or he is pursuing, or he is on a journey, or peradventure he sleepeth, and must be awakened': Bible, I Kings 18:27

          sins of the fathers   Bible, Exodus 20:5

PHASE THE SECOND – MAIDEN NO MORE

CHAPTER 12

- Several weeks later Tess spurns Alec and goes home.

Tess walks home early one Sunday morning, some four months after her arrival at Trantridge. Alec catches her up, berates her for sneaking off and offers her a lift. During the conversation that follows, he admits that he has done wrong, is a 'bad fellow' (p. 125) and offers compensation as he has apparently done before. She refuses his help and goes on alone. Tess meets a labourer whose painted religious slogans sting her conscience. When she gets home, she tells her mother that she should have warned her about men.

COMMENTARY

The end of this chapter was very different in the *Graphic* edition, in which Tess is tricked into a false marriage with Alec. It is worth considering the different moral implications of that association and the rather vaguer relationship that is described in the revised version. The economics of sexual relationships between the classes are made quite explicit in Alec's attempts to help Tess financially and in her refusal, on the grounds that she would then become his 'creature' (p. 125). This offer is essentially reiterated in Chapter 46 and the overall tenor of the conversation repeated several times throughout Phase the Sixth.

The painter of texts appears again in Chapter 44, while Alec is preaching. The red texts themselves act as **metaphorical** moral boundaries – 'THOU, SHALT, NOT, COMMIT' (p. 129) in particular **foreshadows** Tess's later experiences and difficulties. The painter's choice and use of texts suggests a certain emptiness in the rather literal morality of Tess's society.

GLOSSARY

123	serpent hisses where the sweet birds sing Shakespeare, *The Rape of Lucrece*, II, 869–75
126	term statue of Greek god Terminus, placed at boundaries
130	teave (dialect) to toil
	dust and ashes Bible, Genesis 18:27
131	fend hands against (dialect) to guard against
	hontish (dialect) haughty

CHAPTER 13

- Tess, guilty and ashamed, hides indoors during the day and will only go out at dusk.

CHECK THE BOOK

For an analysis of Victorian literary heroines' relationship to spiritual practices, and Tess's inarticulate – almost animalistic – spiritualism in particular, see Diana Basham, *The Trial of Woman: Feminism and the Occult Sciences in Victorian Literature and Society* (Macmillan, 1992).

Tess reflects on her situation. Friends visit her and she goes to church – '[s]he liked to hear the chanting – such as it was – and the old Psalms, and to join in the Morning Hymn' (p. 133) – but, embarrassed by the congregation's gossip, she finally decides to stay home and only ventures out at dusk.

COMMENTARY

Tess seems to shape her own narrative for a while. She bases her story on social convention, in direct opposition to the narrator, who says that she is innocent according to the laws of nature. In this way, having created a certain degree of ambiguity in the last chapter, the narrator clarifies Tess's moral position. This division between culture and nature is what finally tears Tess apart. Her ability to merge with the environment, and her special relationship with the light of dusk – and later, dawn – are recurring motifs.

GLOSSARY

133	Robert South preacher (1634–1716)
	chiming church bells are rung to bring in congregation
134	Langdon English organist (1730–1803) who set Psalm 102 to music

---

CHAPTER 14

- Tess goes out to work.
- But her baby, Sorrow, is weak and dies soon after Tess christens him.

It is harvest time and Tess goes binding. At lunchtime she feeds her baby and the other labourers talk about her sympathetically. She enjoys the work and companionship, and her 'moral sorrows' (p. 142) begin to fade away. Her child, however, is weak, and she returns home to find him very ill. She is worried that he will be damned because he has not been christened. Fearful for his soul, she baptises him herself. She names him Sorrow and he dies in the morning. Tess asks the clergyman if Sorrow will be saved. He assures her that Sorrow's soul is safe, but says he cannot permit the baby to be buried on consecrated ground. Sorrow is buried and Tess tends his grave.

COMMENTARY

The chapter opens with a detached description of the landscape that is typical of Hardy's writing. The binders' gossip is used to comment on Tess's situation, what happened in The Chase and the consequences. The issue of bastardy is touched on here, an ongoing social question for the Victorians, and this coupled with the religious content of the chapter made it deeply controversial. It had to be edited out of the *Graphic* edition. Hardy's ambiguous attitude to modernity can be found in his description of the work being done, which results in the death of '[r]abbits, hares, snakes, rats, mice ... under the teeth of the unerring reaper, and ... the sticks and stones of the harvesters' (p. 137).

GLOSSARY

136	heliolatries forms of sun-worship
	Maltese cross cross of four equal arms, each widening towards the end

continued

> **CONTEXT**
>
> Cyrus McCormick's horse-drawn reaping machine was displayed in 1851 at the Great Exhibition and was subsequently widely adopted by farmers, thereby largely displacing the work of human reapers and harvesters who, though they no longer used sickles or scythes to cut it, nonetheless still had to bind the corn by hand.

📺 CHECK THE FILM

For his 1979 film *Tess* Roman Polanski spent a lot of time recreating historically accurate locations using livestock, furniture and costumes that were of the period, and finding places that mirrored Hardy's landscape. The original novel is set in Wessex, i.e. Dorset, however, whereas Polanski filmed his adaptation in Normandy, France.

142	gold-leaf halo … saint medieval Italian paintings of saints
143	burn the damned are burnt in hell
	Aholah and Aholibah two harlots, punished by God: Bible, Ezekiel 23
	no salvation Older interpretations of Christian doctrine dictated that only those who have been baptised may enter heaven
145	a phrase … Genesis Bible, Genesis 3:16 or Genesis 35:18
	stopt-diapason pipe-organ note; like a flute

CHAPTER 15

- Tess decides to move on.

Time passes and, as Tess reflects on her life, she comes to understand her mortality. She decides to go somewhere where she can start afresh, and 'On one point she was resolved: there should be no more d'Urberville air-castles in the dreams and deeds of her new life. She would be the dairymaid Tess, and nothing more' (p. 151).

COMMENTARY

This chapter focuses on Tess's thoughts and feelings, sets up the terms for the next section and ties up the second phase. Time and Tess's movement into adulthood are both represented by the passage of the seasons. This links Tess with nature as she sets out to recoup her lost innocence.

GLOSSARY

149	Roger Ascham author (1515–68); from *The Scholemaster*, 1570
	Saint Augustine an early founder of the Church (354–430); from *Confessions*, Book 10, Chapter 29
150	Jeremy Taylor an English divine (1613–67); from *Holy Dying*, 1651

PHASE THE THIRD – THE RALLY

CHAPTER 16

- Two to three years after her return from Trantridge, Tess leaves home to work as a milkmaid at Talbothays.

 CHECK THE BOOK

It is 'a thyme-scented, bird-hatching morning in May' (p. 155) and Tess, now a young woman of twenty, leaves home for the second time. As soon as she reaches the Valley of the Great Dairies her spirits rise and she is moved to song. It is milking time and Tess follows the cows to Talbothays.

COMMENTARY

Tess's feelings are often reflected by her environment. The pleasant vale echoes Tess's new-found happiness, which resonates in the lush surroundings and bright May sunshine. Music, in the form of song, continues to be an important theme.

Jeff Nunokawa argues that Hardy's descriptions, such as his description of 'the Valley of the Great Dairies' (p. 156), frequently present the reader with the kind of spectacle more commonly found in nineteenth-century tour guides. See his 'Tess, tourism, and the spectacle of the woman' in Linda M. Shires, ed., *Rewriting the Victorians: Theory, History and the Politics of Gender* (Routledge, 1992).

GLOSSARY		
156	Van Alsloot	Denis van Alsloot (1570–1626) Flemish landscape painter
	Sallaert	Anthonis Sallaert (1590–1657/8) Flemish painter of everyday life
157	the Evangelist	John the Baptist, who sees the River of Life in a vision: Bible, Revelation 22:1
158	she had eaten ... knowledge	Bible, Genesis 3, Adam and Eve are expelled from the garden of Eden when they eat the forbidden fruit from the tree of knowledge
	'O ye Sun and Moon ...'	taken from the Order for Morning Prayer in the Book of Common Prayer
159	steading	outbuilding
	barton	farmyard
	milchers	cows giving milk
160	Olympian shapes ... Pharaohs	refers to figures picked out in friezes in ancient Greece, Rome and Egypt

CHAPTER 17

- Tess begins to work.
- Angel Clare is asked to play his harp to the cows.

Tess introduces herself to the master-dairyman and sets to work. The cows seem reluctant to give down their milk, so the milkmaids and men begin to sing. Someone suggests that one of the men should play his harp. Dairyman Dick tells a story about William Dewy, who played his fiddle to get away from a bull. Tess recognises the owner of the harp as the man who did not dance with her at the club-walking. When she goes to bed, the other milkmaids tell her about Mr Angel Clare, a clergyman's son who is learning about farming.

COMMENTARY

Key characters are introduced for the third phase. Class differences are made explicit in the use of 'sir'. As Clare is brought in, links are made between this chapter and earlier passages. The scene seems timeless, but it is clear that the landscape is, and always has been, in flux, 'compounded of old landscapes long forgotten' (p. 163), while the fact that William Dewy – a character from *Under the Greenwood Tree* (1872) – is buried in Mellstock churchyard gives added depth to Hardy's Wessex.

CONTEXT
The Low Church was the evangelical branch of the Anglican Church, where worship was characterised by very little ceremony and concentration on preaching. The High Church, established by the Anglican 'Oxford movement' (1833–45), revived the ceremonies and rituals of the early Church, and set up Anglican religious communities.

GLOSSARY

161	pattens wooden overshoes, clogs
	pinner pinafore
	broad-cloth thick black material
	terminatively in conclusion
162	cowcumber (dialect) cucumber
	kex dry, hollow stem of umbelliferous plant
164	nott (dialect) without horns
	stave line of music, therefore song
	tranters irregular carriers of goods

164	do ye mind do you remember
165	leery (dialect) empty, hungry
167	stuff woollen material
	leads lead milk pans
168	wrings cheese presses

CHAPTER 18

- We are introduced to Angel Clare.

Angel Clare has rejected the key tenets of his father's Anglican faith, so Mr Clare has refused to send him to university. Angel now lives in the attic of the dairy and eats with the dairyman, his wife and the labourers, whose 'companionship' he takes 'a real delight in' (p. 173). He notices Tess at breakfast.

COMMENTARY

We often find allusions to other texts in *Tess*. As in the previous chapter, here we find Hardy recycling some of his own work, in this case his essay 'The Dorsetshire Labourer' in *Longman's Magazine* (1883). With particular reference to 'Hodge' (p. 173), Hardy would also have been familiar with Richard Jefferies's *Hodge and His Masters* (1880).

The information that Clare had an affair with a woman in London, and the image of the dairyman's knife and fork being poised like gallows pave the way for Chapters 34 and 59 respectively. Clare's first observation of Tess – 'What a fresh and virginal daughter of Nature that milkmaid is!' (p. 176) – is also ominous. Tess speaks almost as a clairvoyant here. '"I don't know about ghosts," she was saying; "but I do know that our souls can be made to go outside our bodies when we are alive"' (p. 175), which **foreshadows** events in Chapter 55.

QUESTION

Consider the interplay of faith and doubt in nineteenth-century literature with particular reference to *Tess of the d'Urbervilles*.

CONTEXT

There was considerable interest in mysticism and spiritualism in the latter half of the nineteenth century among the educated, artistic and professional middle and upper-middle classes, both as entertainment and as philosophy. One of the most famous mediums and founder of the Theosophical Society, Madame Blavatsky, died in 1891. Followers of theosophy included Annie Besant, the social reformer and leader of the 1888 'Match Girls' Strike'; believers in spiritualism included Arthur Conan Doyle and Elizabeth Barrett Browning. Critics included George Eliot and Robert Browning.

GLOSSARY

170 **redemptive theolatry** Christian belief that salvation was achieved through Christ's sacrifice

171 **thimble-riggers** cheats

Evangelical teaches the word of the Christian Bible, and belief in salvation through faith

'Indeed opine …' Robert Browning, *Easter Day*, 8

Article Four clergymen had to subscribe to the 'Thirty-Nine Articles' of the Anglican Church to be ordained. The fourth relates to Christ's resurrection

'the removing …' Bible, Hebrews 12:27

173 **Hodge** peasant

Pascal French philosopher (1623–62), 'The sharper one's mind, the more one notices how many original men there are'

Miltonic … Cromwellian reference to Thomas Gray's 'Elegy Written in a Country Churchyard'

174 **road to dusty death** Shakespeare, *Macbeth*, Act V Scene 5

mess eat together

CHAPTER 19

- Angel plays his harp and Tess becomes entranced.

Angel begins to herd the cows so that Tess gets the easiest ones to milk. Having been embarrassed by complaining about this, she goes for a walk after work. While she is out she hears Angel playing his harp and becomes fascinated. When he stops they get into a slightly awkward conversation. He is puzzled by her bitterness; she is confused by his interest in farming. As time passes, though, they get to know each other a little better.

COMMENTARY

This chapter establishes the terms of Tess and Angel's relationship. They idealise each other – he sees her as a simple 'daughter of the soil' (p. 183), she sees him as an 'intelligence' (p. 181). The references to Tess's difficulty in describing her experiences, the spirit of the age and 'the ache of modernism' (p. 180) are suggestive of Hardy's interest in modernity. But we also see how Tess is subject to and driven by nature's rhythms. Tess is described animalistically, first as a bird – reminding us of Chapter 9 – then as a cat. The garden's red stains, sticky profusion and clouds of pollen – echoing the clouds of dust in the barn at Chaseborough in Chapter 10 – are symbolic of abundant fertility, desire and insemination.

CHECK THE BOOK

Marjorie Garson suggests in *Hardy's Fables of Integrity: Woman, Body, Text* (Clarendon Press, 1991) that the sultry description of nature in the garden is only effective because the sexual nature of Angel and Tess's relationship is otherwise repressed.

GLOSSARY

179	**cuckoo-spittle** frothy insect secretion
	blights mildew
	madder stains a crimson dye; in earlier editions it reads 'blood-red stains'
	apple-blooth (dialect) apple blossom
180	**hobble** (dialect) predicament
181	**Valley of Humiliation** John Bunyan (1628–88), *The Pilgrim's Progress*
	man of Uz Job, biblical figure who suffered extreme torment: Job 7:15–16
	Peter the Great Tsar Peter I (1672–1725), disguised, studied in Dutch and English shipyards
	Abraham biblical figure, possessed many animals and servants: Genesis 30:25–43
	Andean like the Andes, South American mountains
182	**'lords and ladies'** small lilies
	Queen of Sheba biblical figure awed by Solomon's wealth and wisdom: I Kings 10:4–5
	shine on the just … alike Bible, Matthew 5:45
183	*niaiseries* (French) foolishness
	rozums (dialect) quaint saying or nonsense; someone with strange ideas
184	**in Palestine** on the medieval crusades

CHAPTER 20

- Tess and Angel begin to fall in love.

Tess is very happy at the dairy: 'She was, for one thing, physically and mentally suited among these new surroundings' (p. 185). She and Clare often meet before sunrise when they go out to milk. He calls her Demeter and Artemis, while she insists that he call her Tess.

COMMENTARY

This is a brief, but dense and highly suspenseful chapter. As in the rest of the novel, Hardy reminds his readers, and makes extensive use of, earlier scenes, to draw on Tess's relationship with Alec. Hardy's use of figures from classical myth parallels his earlier description of the Chaseborough folk dance. The fog and dewdrops on her lashes echo the scene in The Chase. Tess's state of mind contrasts with her feelings in Chapter 13. She is idealised by Clare so that, echoing her comments in Chapter 18, she becomes less and less real for him; 'a soul at large', she metamorphoses into 'a visionary essence of woman' (p. 187).

The dawn, which stands poised on the threshold of night and day, reflects the way their relationship is also poised and about to change. The potential for an Edenic fall is highlighted by reference to Adam and Eve. The source of the fall, original sin, and the complexity of Tess's moral position in respect of this is in turn indicated through the narrator's reference to Mary Magdalene.

CONTEXT

For the Victorians there was a binary opposition between 'virgin' and 'whore', or the Madonna and Mary Magdalene.

GLOSSARY

185	*convenances* (French) social customs
	aborescence growth of trees
186	as if they were Adam and Eve another reference to Genesis
187	Resurrection hour time when Christ is supposed to have risen from the dead

> 187   Magdalen Mary Magdalene, out of whom Christ had cast
>   seven devils, was the first to see him resurrected, Mark
>   16:9. In art she is usually represented as a prostitute
>   **Artemis** Greek goddess of hunting and chastity
>   **Demeter** Greek goddess of the fruits of the earth

CHAPTER 21

- Tess is reminded of her past.
- She thinks about marriage.

While the dairyfolk wait for the butter to form, they speculate that someone is in love, and dairyman Dick tells a story about a young man, Jack Dollop, who had to hide in the churn to avoid his prospective mother-in-law. Tess is deeply affected by the story, and as she leaves the dairy the butter comes. That evening she overhears the other dairymaids, Retty Priddle, Izz Huett and Marian talking about Angel Clare. Tess believes that she should never marry, yet she is drawn into thinking about the possibility.

COMMENTARY

Tess has clearly fallen in love with Angel, yet we are reminded, just as Tess is, of the impossibility of her situation: 'ought she to do this?' (p. 194). The use of superstition and folk stories can be compared with the references to classical myth in previous chapters.

CONTEXT

Angel is planning on taking on a ten-thousand-acre colonial cattle farm and therefore needs a practical wife. It was relatively common for the younger sons of the well-to-do to invest and become involved in livestock farming in Australia, Canada, the United States and South America in the nineteenth century.

GLOSSARY

> 189   **Conjuror** tells fortunes and cures ills; Trendle appears in
>   Hardy's 'The Withered Arm', Fall appears in *The Mayor
>   of Casterbridge*
>   **cast folk's waters** tells fortunes from urine (this does not
>   appear in all editions)
>   **touchwood** fungus infested, dry wood
>
>   continued

190	Holy Thursday a rarely used name for Ascension Day, the day Christ ascended into heaven
	ballyragging scolding or abusing
	by side and by seam in all kinds of ways (this does not appear in all editions)
191	pummy (dialect) crushed apples for cider-making
	dog-days late summer; hottest part of year

CHAPTER 22

- Tess tries to get Angel to take notice of the other girls.

The butter has a tang of garlic and everyone has to go out to pull up the offending weed. Tess uses the opportunity to divert Clare and get him to look at the other dairywomen.

COMMENTARY

This a very carefully written chapter which generates a feeling of tension and suspense reflecting Tess's increasing anxiety about her relationship with Clare. Tess lives up to the Victorian feminine ideal of self-sacrifice here, but we are reminded that she is also sensitive to quite unfeminine sexual needs and desires. The sentence 'Angel Clare had the honour of all the dairymaids in his keeping' (p. 197), in other words, they would all have offered themselves to him if he had asked them to, becomes pertinent later.

CHAPTER 23

- On their way to church Tess and the other dairymaids find the road flooded.
- Angel saves the day.

It is now July. The dairymaids are all on their way to church, but it has been raining and 'the result of the rain had been to flood the

CONTEXT

Attending church or chapel was a way in which young people could legitimately socialise at this time, and it was the one day of the week when they could dress up. Hence Hardy's observation that Sunday is a 'day of vanity ... when flesh went forth to coquet with flesh while hypocritically affecting business with spiritual things' (p. 199).

lane over-shoe to a distance of some fifty yards' (p. 199). Angel finds them stranded and carries each one across. He and Tess establish an understanding. At first the other dairymaids are jealous, but when Tess tells them that she cannot marry him, they make up.

COMMENTARY

In the censored *Graphic* version Angel carts the dairymaids through the water in a wheelbarrow. We see the dairymaids as Angel does and we begin to understand the passion he is developing for Tess. The chapter is highly charged. Notice the insects trapped in their skirts and the drip, drip of the cheese press. Angel and Alec are represented as opposites – when Angel is cheek to cheek with Tess he restrains himself.

GLOSSARY

200	That-it-may-please-Thees from the Anglican morning service, part of the Litany
	un-Sabbatarian it was customary to wear one's best clothes on Sunday
	thistlespud spade for rooting up thistles
	sermons in stones buildings, Shakespeare, *As You Like It*, Act II Scene 1
201	A time to embrace Bible, Ecclesiastes 3:5
202	paltered become evasive
	Three Leahs to get one Rachel after working for seven years to marry Rachel, Jacob is tricked into marrying her sister Leah and then has to work another seven years to earn Rachel's hand: Bible, Genesis 29
206	thorny crown echoes the crown of thorns placed on Christ before the crucifixion

? QUESTION

To what extent does *Tess of the d'Urbervilles* suggest that masculinity and femininity are cultural constructs?

CHAPTER 24

- Angel confesses his love for Tess.

Clare, mesmerised by Tess's beauty, betrays himself by suddenly embracing her: 'Resolutions, reticences, prudences, fears fell back …

and … [he] went quickly towards the desire of his eyes' (p. 209). He stops short of a kiss, but declares his love.

COMMENTARY

This chapter brings the third phase to a close. Clare's love is cultured, restrained, even in the heat of passion, unlike Alec's. The embrace takes place in the middle of the day at the height of summer, in contrast to the midnight scene in The Chase – a scene that is echoed by Tess's tears. The oppressive heat tells us a lot about the nature of Angel and Tess's love. It is **ironic** that he loves Tess's physical flaws, but comes to detest her moral imperfections.

> **CONTEXT**
>
> The French Revolutionary calendar (adopted October 1793) consisted of twelve months of thirty days each (starting 22 September by the old calendar), given descriptive names: Vendémiaire (vintage), Brumaire (mist), Frimaire (frost), Nivôse (snow), Pluviôse (rain), Ventôse (wind), Germinal (seed), Floréal (blossom), Prairial (meadow), Messidor (harvest), Thermidor (heat), Fructidor (fruits). The remaining five or six days were called *Sans-culottides* and were to be national holidays. Each month was divided into three ten-day weeks, with one day of rest. Abandoned by Napoleon I, it made a brief reappearance under the Paris Commune of 1871.

> **GLOSSARY**
>
> | | |
> |---|---|
> | 207 | **Thermidorean** 19 July to 17 August, from French Revolutionary calendar |
> | 208 | **diurnal roll** daily turning of the earth, echoes William Wordsworth's 'Lucy' poem 'A slumber did my …' |
> | | **cameo** relief carving in stone, often of two layers in different colours, the lower a background for the other |
> | 209 | **Elizabethan simile** common comparison found in Elizabethan poetry |
> | | *aura* (Latin) breath, breeze |

PHASE THE FOURTH – THE CONSEQUENCE

CHAPTER 25

- Angel visits his family.

Clare contemplates the consequences of his actions and decides to go home to talk to his family. On the way he meets Miss Mercy Chant, whom his parents want him to marry. When he reaches the vicarage he feels that he no longer fits in: 'A prig would have said

that he had lost culture, and a prude that he had become coarse'
(p. 219).

COMMENTARY

This chapter focuses entirely on Clare, his motivations and feelings.
His father seems more generous and forgiving than his brothers, a
fact which is reiterated in Chapter 44. The chapter as a whole lays
the ground for Angel's responses and actions later in the novel.
Angel's life at Talbothays is in striking contrast to that of his family;
the natural life of the farm is opposed to the cultured life of the
vicarage.

**CHECK
THE BOOK**

In *The English Novel
from Dickens to
Lawrence* (Hogarth,
1984), Raymond
Williams argues that
Tess is a novel that
is about what he
calls the 'border
country … between
custom and
education, between
work and ideas,
between love
of place and
experience of
change' (Chapter 4,
p. 98).

GLOSSARY

213	noctambulist walker at night
	Walt Whitman American poet (1819–92); from 'Crossing the Brooklyn Ferry'
214	the creeper blushed possibly a Virginia creeper
	pachydermatous thick-skinned, like an elephant
	heterodoxy unconventional belief
	First Cause that which set the universe in motion
216	'pleasure girdled about with pain' A. C. Swinburne, *Atalanta in Calydon*
217	Antinomianism belief that moral law is unimportant compared with faith in Christ
	court-patched society ladies used to wear small black patches as facial adornment
	Wycliffe, Huss, Luther, Calvin these men established Protestant Reformation from the fourteenth to the sixteenth centuries
218	Christiad … Pauliad epics of the lives of Christ and Paul, derived from *Iliad*
	determinism belief that the way one lives one's life does not affect one's salvation, which is already determined by God
	Schopenhauer and Leopardi early nineteenth-century German and Italian pessimistic writers. Schopenhauer was a philosopher; Leopardi was a poet
	Canons laws of the Anglican Church

continued

218	Rubric directions for the conduct of divine service
	Articles Articles of Religion: doctrinal base of the Anglican Church
	geocentric belief that the earth is at the centre of the universe
219	hall-marked mark that guarantees purity of precious metals
	Correggio Italian painter (1494–1534)
	Velasquez Spanish painter (1599–1660)
	Diocesan Synod assembly of clergymen
	Visitations inspections of diocese by bishop
220	high thinking ... living see William Wordsworth's sonnet 'O Friend! I know not which way I must look'
221	*dapes inemptae* (Latin) unbought meal
	delirium tremens trembling suffered by heavy drinkers

CHAPTER 26

- Angel talks with his parents about marrying Tess.

Angel talks to his parents about Tess. On the way back to Talbothays, his father talks to Clare about his ministry, and how he has often been insulted; once 'a young upstart squire named d'Urberville' (p. 227) gave him a barracking. Angel refers to a legend: the d'Urberville coach.

CONTEXT

Calvinistic doctrine refers to Calvinism, a strict form of Protestant Christian doctrine linked to Puritanism.

COMMENTARY

We already know about Mr Clare's preaching near Trantridge from Chapter 12 and the affair between Clare's father and Alec is picked up in Chapter 45; the legend about the coach is explained in Chapters 33 and 51. The reference to Alec reminds us of the past and foreshadows later events.

GLOSSARY

223	**goings-out and your comings-in** Bible, Psalms 121:8
224	**vestal** virgin who tended the Roman temple of Vesta
227	**Christologist** student of theology of Christ's life
	'exclaim against ... succession' Shakespeare, *Hamlet*, Act II Scene 2
228	**'Thou fool ... of thee!'** Bible, Luke 12:20
	'Being reviled ... unto this day' Bible, I Corinthians 4:12–14

CHAPTER 27

- On his return, Angel proposes to Tess.
- She refuses him.

That afternoon Angel proposes to Tess as they work in the dairy. Tess says she cannot become his wife because of the differences in their station. Angel distracts her from her distress by recounting the story of his father and Alec d'Urberville. Tess is therefore reminded about her past and this guarantees her second refusal at the end of the chapter.

COMMENTARY

This chapter contrasts sharply with the previous two. Tess is described animalistically – among other things she is snake-like – and Hardy again draws on the story of Adam and Eve: 'she regarded him as Eve at her second waking might have regarded Adam' (p. 232). The narrative focuses in particular on the redness of Tess's mouth when she yawns, and the way the sun catches her veins. Tess is as frightened by Angel's passion, like Michael's flaming sword, as she was by Alec's devilish seduction.

 CHECK THE BOOK

For a discussion of Darwin's influence on Hardy, and Hardy's use of different (e.g. time- and visual-) scales and multiple plots, see Gillian Beer, *Darwin's Plots: Evolutionary Narrative in Darwin, George Eliot and Nineteenth-Century Fiction* (second edition, Cambridge University Press, 2000).

CONTEXT

Pantheism is a **metaphysical** and religious position which sees God in everything, or more precisely believes that 'God is everything and everything is God' – see H. P. Owen, *Concepts of Deity* (Macmillan, 1971), p. 74 – and which perceives everything as unified, and this unity as being divine.

GLOSSARY

232   fibrils small threads

        Eve at her second waking after she has slept: Genesis

234   Tractarian Oxford movement published their ideas as *Tracts for the Times*

        'Leave ... days' Alfred Tennyson, *In Memoriam*

CHAPTER 28

- Angel proposes again.
- Tess refuses again.

Tess's conscience continues to make her resist Angel, because, she says, 'I am not good enough – not worthy enough' (p. 237), and she says she will give him her reasons that Sunday. When he kisses her arm Tess, overwrought and unequal to this moral struggle, runs away to a small wood and misses the milking. She fears that she will give way.

COMMENTARY

Tess's simple charms are contrasted sharply with the flirtatious urban women Clare already knows, yet she is becoming more cultured as she associates with him. Tess's flight to the wood is like that in Chapter 42.

GLOSSARY

237   trowing (archaism) believing, being aware

        'sigh gratis' echo of Shakespeare, *Hamlet*, Act II Scene 2; means to sigh without hope of reward

        carking possibly 'worrying'

240   loving satire Angel cannot believe that Tess has had 'experiences' and therefore he makes fun of her

        convolvulus climbing plant

PHASE THE FOURTH – THE CONSEQUENCE

CHAPTER 29

- Tess refuses Angel again.
- However, this time she admits that she loves him.

On Sunday morning dairyman Dick tells everyone the recent history of Jack Dollop, who, among other things, married a widow for her fifty pounds a year, which she then lost by marrying him. This leads to the comment by Mrs Crick that 'the silly body [Jack Dollop's wife] should have told en sooner that the ghost of her first man would trouble him' (p. 243). Tess is thrown by this so that she does not tell Angel her story. A fortnight goes by. Then, after refusing him again, she finally admits to Clare that she loves him. They drive the milk to the station.

COMMENTARY

Tess and Angel's relationship blossomed and matured as spring became summer, they courted at dawn and now at the autumn equinox everything hangs in the balance. Angel woos Tess among the brooding and farrowing animals and his desire for her leads him to pursue her, almost as Alec did. The end of the chapter is a cliffhanger.

GLOSSARY

244   scram (dialect) puny, weak, feeble

CONTEXT

In the late nineteenth century, demand for milk in urban areas remained high. Between 1860 and 1900 annual milk consumption rose from approximately six hundred million gallons to eight hundred and thirty gallons nationally, and individual consumption rose from nine gallons a year to fifteen gallons. This allowed farmers in dairying counties like Dorset to use the improved communications of the Great Western Railway to offset agricultural depression.

CHAPTER 30

- Tess finally accepts Angel's proposal.

On the way to the station they pass an old manor house that belonged to the d'Urbervilles. On the way back Tess tries to tell Angel her story, but she falters, and finally accepts his proposal.

CONTEXT

In the story of Pygmalion an artist (Pygmalion) falls in love with a marble statue that he has carved. His love is so strong that the Roman goddess Venus brings the statue to life. This myth was represented by the Pre-Raphaelite Edward Burne-Jones in four paintings entitled *Pygmalion and the Image* (1878).

COMMENTARY

This is another turning point in Tess's life; many earlier events are recalled and future incidents foreshadowed in this chapter. Tess and Angel talk about the stars like Tess and her brother in Chapter 4. The drive is reminiscent of her ride with Alec and her journey at night with Prince. They pass the manor house where they will spend their honeymoon and where Angel will find out that Tess is not so childlike as he thought. The striking image of the train has parallels with the threshing scene in Chapter 47. The engagement takes place at dusk, and though Tess fails to narrate her story to Angel we remember it all too well. The fact that Angel says Tess's 'arms are like wet marble' (p. 250) implies that he sees in her the embodiment of perfected and objectified femininity, and makes oblique reference to the story of Pygmalion.

GLOSSARY

250	Caroline of the reign of Charles I and II
251	centurions officers of the Roman army
255	lucubrations night-time meditations

CHAPTER 31

- Joan Durbeyfield advises Tess to keep quiet about her past.
- Tess, however, is not so sure.

Tess writes to her mother, who advises her not to confess. The engagement continues through October and Angel insists on setting a date for the wedding. Tess is happy, but when the others surprise them and are told of the betrothal the generosity of the dairymaids makes her want to tell all, 'rather than preserve a silence which might be deemed a treachery to him, and which somehow seemed a wrong to these' (p. 265).

COMMENTARY

We are warned that Angel is probably not so forgiving as Tess thinks. The dangers of the excessive idealisation of the other to which both Tess and Angel succumb are highlighted. The image of mist and drops of water on Tess's lashes occurs again here, reminding us of The Chase. The letter gives Joan her own voice.

GLOSSARY

256	J old form of letter I, demonstrates Joan's piecemeal education
257	guide, philosopher, and friend Alexander Pope, *Essay on Man*, IV
	Byronic Lord Byron (1788–1824), a Romantic poet who celebrated sensuality
	Shelleyan Percy Bysshe Shelley (1792–1822), a Romantic poet who celebrated the spiritual
258	champaign open country
260	photosphere glow around stars
	true, and honest … good report Bible, Philippians 4:8
261	springe trap
	dogs metal supports for burning wood
263	baily bailiff, farm manager

CHAPTER 32

- Angel and Tess name the day.

Angel presses Tess to name the day. The last day of December is set and things move along quickly. Angel chooses the old d'Urberville manor house for their honeymoon, on the pretext that he can then visit a neighbouring mill.

CONTEXT

'That never … done amiss' (p. 272) is a version of 'The Boy and the Mantle' – in this ballad, a dress which changes colour to reveal unfaithfulness is taken to the court of King Arthur; when Queen Guinevere puts it on, it reveals her adultery with Lancelot.

COMMENTARY

This is a fast chapter. Things move along quickly giving a sense of undue haste, and 'Tess was now carried along' (p. 269). The fleeting transitions of time and nature, as seen in the passing glory of the gnats, are highlighted. Clare is acting quite recklessly, and he knows it. Tess's fears, alongside her sense of fatalism, add to the tension.

GLOSSARY

270	bolting sifting flour
271	banns the three weeks before a church wedding the names of the prospective couple are read out, unless they have a special licence

CHECK THE NET

Search the Internet for Mitsuharu Matsuoka's Hyper-Concordance at the Victorian Literary Studies Archive, an excellent online resource where you can do word searches of the text.

CHAPTER 33

- Tess tries to confess to Angel in a letter, but he never receives it.
- They are married, but bad omens abound.

Tess and Angel spend Christmas Eve together. While they are in town, a man recognises Tess and passes comment. Angel hits him, but things are smoothed over and they return home. That night he dreams about the fight and Tess resolves to tell him about her past in a letter. When the wedding day arrives, Tess discovers that he never received her confession, 'owing to her having in her haste thrust it beneath the carpet as well as beneath the door' (p. 277). They are married and Tess is blissfully happy, but as they leave a cock crows – a bad omen.

COMMENTARY

A doom-laden chapter in which Tess is beleaguered by omens, including the spectre of the d'Urberville coach from Chapter 26, much reduced like the family itself. The focus is as much on the grotesque (including the nauseating coachman), as it is on the happy event.

GLOSSARY	
273	negatived ... forthwith i.e. denied she was a virgin
275	drachm small weight
276	blower material fixed to increase the draught
	gieing a rattling good randy (dialect) giving a boisterous party
277	temerarious rash
278	close carriage carriage with roof
	post-chaise travelling reference to coaching which predates railway travel
	felloes wheel-rims
279	*partie carrée* (French) party of four
280	angel ... sun Bible, Revelation 19:17 (this does not appear in all editions)
281	Friar Laurence the young couple's helper in *Romeo and Juliet*

CONTEXT

It was customary in the nineteenth century for church bells to be rung in order to call their congregations to services. The English tradition is to use 'change ringing', i.e. the bells are rung in such a way that the order in which they are sounded changes. Chapter 33 refers to a 'modest peal of three notes' (p. 279) because the church is only large enough to carry or afford three bells; wealthier churches had six or even eight bells.

CHAPTER 34

- That night, Angel tells Tess of an early misdemeanour.
- She now feels confident enough to tell him her story.

Tess and Clare drive to the manor at Wellbridge. As they go up to their rooms they see the life-size portraits of two d'Urberville ladies. While they wait for their luggage Tess tries on some jewels left to Clare's wife by his godmother. Angel is impressed, but, he says, 'I think I love you best in the wing-bonnet and cotton-frock' (p. 288). When their clothes arrive Tess and Angel hear that Retty has tried to drown herself, Marian is drunk and Izz is depressed. Tess becomes determined to confess. As soon as Clare has finished his own disclosure, she begins to recite her story.

COMMENTARY

The chapter moves back and forth between description and dialogue, which generates considerable suspense. The way in which Clare resorts to scripture when telling his story indicates that he is still quite bound by convention. Alec also likes her in a wing-bonnet, and declares in Chapter 47: 'you field-girls should never wear those bonnets if you wish to keep out of danger' (p. 409). The consequences of Tess's confession are hinted at in the description of the lurid fire, by the shadow which she casts and the way in which she takes up the mantle of the awful d'Urberville women. The phase ends on a cliffhanger.

CONTEXT

A trencher was originally a kind of bread as a plate on which cut meat was served. It was probably only used in the medieval period at feasts, when several fresh trenchers would be needed for elaborate meals. They would be pre-made for important guests, but trenchers could also be cut as thick slices from ordinary loaves as needed. A 'trencher-woman' (p. 289) as used here is a woman who eats meat, or a stout woman.

GLOSSARY

288	crush social gathering
	gallied (dialect) scared
289	mops and brooms ... 'em probably, senseless from drink
	withy-bed willow plantation
	traps personal possessions
290	night-rail (dialect) nightdress
291	Aldebaran ... Sirius bright stars that emit coloured flashes; Sirius is ill-omened
292	plenary inspirations belief the Scriptural writers were inspired by the word of God and that the Bible is therefore infallibly true
	words of Paul Bible, I Timothy 4:12
	'Integer Vitae' (Latin) wholeness of life: Horace, Odes, Book I, Ode 22
	a certain place ... good intentions proverb
	Last Day luridness on the last day the world will be consumed by fire: Bible, Revelation 16:8

PHASE THE FIFTH – THE WOMAN PAYS

CHAPTER 35

- Angel rejects Tess.

Tess finishes her story. Clare is horror-stricken and no longer sees Tess as the woman, nor as the 'new-sprung child of nature' (p. 302), he loved; she can say nothing to console him. When Clare goes out she follows him and they walk slowly around the village until he tells her to return to their lodgings. When Angel gets back he is reminded of Tess by the portraits of the d'Urberville women. They sleep in separate beds.

COMMENTARY

This chapter is pivotal and highlights the key concerns of the text. Here we see the consequences of Tess and Angel's idealising love. Repetition is used to intensify feeling, while the cottager's observation makes Tess and Angel's walk feel drawn out. The rest of the world seems indifferent to their plight. The ruined abbey symbolises the decline of conventional morality, but this slightly gothic detail also adds to the feeling that Angel is haunted by the spectre of simple Tessy, grotesquely transformed into a delinquent aristocrat. The dialogue feels contrived at times; the 'O's and 'Ah's add a melodramatic touch. But, also notice subtle details like Angel's tear, and how ordinary objects and everyday things like the fire are transformed by Tess's confession.

> **? QUESTION**
>
> Examine the theme of sexual morality in the novel. If there is a double standard at work, how might this be interpreted?

GLOSSARY

299–300	good-hussif hussif, case for carrying needles and thread (this does not appear in all editions)
300	*Agape* (Greek) a love-feast held by early Christians in memory of the Lord's Supper
301	'Behold when thy face … pain' A. C. Swinburne, *Atalanta in Calydon*

continued

302	more sinned against than sinning Shakespeare, *King Lear*, Act III Scene 2
304	tester of white dimity canopy of white cotton
	mistletoe supposed to bring good luck and fertility
305	passion's slave Shakespeare, *Hamlet*, Act III Scene 2
306	The little less ... away! Robert Browning, 'By the Fireside'

CONTEXT

Civil divorce courts were established in England and Wales with the Matrimonial Causes Act 1857, which also gave women custody rights for the first time. However, women only had limited access to divorce; though a husband could apply for divorce on the grounds of adultery, a wife could only do so on the grounds of her husband having committed bigamy, rape, sodomy, bestiality, cruelty or desertion. Divorce was also expensive and still really limited to the wealthy; only 582 people had divorced by 1900.

CHAPTER 36

- Angel cannot accept Tess as his wife.
- Nevertheless, he will not divorce her.

In the morning Angel goes to work at the mill and the next three days pass quietly. Tess hopes that Clare will forgive her, but it gradually becomes apparent that he cannot and she suggests that she return to her family. Clare observes that he is likely to love her better in her absence.

COMMENTARY

In this chapter both Tess's and Angel's faults are considered. The fact that their affection differs is stressed and this echoes what was said about the nature of their love towards the end of the last phase, but Tess's purity is maintained by the narrator – she is not artful or sophisticated enough to manipulate Clare – and the possibility that Clare will return to her is hinted at. Does she get the idea of murdering Alec from Clare's suggestion 'If he were dead it might be different ...' (p. 313)?

GLOSSARY

| 312 | she sought not her own ... provoked Bible, I Corinthians 13:5 |
| 313 | endure the ills ... fly to others Shakespeare, *Hamlet*, Act III Scene 1 |

> 314   **M. Sully-Prudhomme** French poet (1839–1907) who
> excelled in describing delicate emotions
>
> 315   **The intuitive heart of woman ... bitterness** Bible, Proverbs
> 14:10

CHAPTER 37

- Angel carries Tess to a stone coffin in his sleep.
- They separate.

Angel, sleepwalking and murmuring, 'Dead! dead! dead!' (p. 317),
takes Tess out of her room and lays her in an abbot's stone coffin.
Tess leads him back without waking him. He remembers nothing
the next day. They visit Talbothays. He gives her fifty pounds, tells
her not to write and they part as planned.

COMMENTARY

A highly sensational chapter which is marked by exciting incidents
and strong uncomplicated feelings, though unlike a **melodramatic**
text it does not have a happy ending. Angel's true feelings are
revealed. The changes in their relationship are reflected in the
turbulent waters of the river and are highlighted by the memories
conjured up when they visit the Cricks. The pity and sadness that
are aroused, and the **pathos** of Tess being put in the abbot's tomb,
prefigure her and Angel's arrival at Stonehenge in Chapter 58 and
seem to play on fantastic and eerie, **gothic** motifs.

**CHECK
THE FILM**
Roman Polanski's
1979 adaptation
relied on the
camerawork
of British
cinematographer
Geoffrey Unsworth,
who died during its
shooting, for much
of its atmosphere
and effect. Polanski
himself was well
aware of the
melodramatic
elements in Hardy's
text.

GLOSSARY

321   **Samson shaking himself** Bible, Judges 16:20

325   **'God's not ... world!'** adapted from Robert Browning,
Pippa Passes, Part I, 'Morning'

CHAPTER 38

- Tess returns home.
- Ashamed, she pretends she and Angel are reconciled, and leaves.

Tess returns home, but on the way is embarrassed to hear the story of her own marriage. Her mother tells her off for confessing and when she overhears her father doubting the validity of the ceremony she decides to leave as soon as possible. When a letter comes from Angel, in 'her craving for the lustre of her true position as his wife, and to hide from her parents the vast extent of the division between them' (p. 330), she pretends that they are reconciled, gives her mother half of the money Angel has left her and goes. Her father has sold the horse Alec sent him and we are told that her family will spend the money on the strength of her more recent good fortune.

QUESTION

Consider Tess's interactions with her family and community, at each return, and the decisions Tess makes. Does she have too much pride?

COMMENTARY

Tess's second return home, similar to that in Chapter 12, creates a symmetrical structure in the novel. At home, Tess drops Angel's more cultured language. Whereas her parents are selfish, Tess is prideful, as we were reminded in the last chapter.

GLOSSARY		
327	Nation	damnation
329	unceiled	without a ceiling
330	glane	(dialect) to leer, to sneer

CHAPTER 39

- Angel determines to go to Brazil.

Three weeks after the separation, Clare goes back to Emminster. He has decided to emigrate and tells his parents that he has left

Tess with her family while he visits Brazil. Stung by his mother's innocent questions, he is unable to forget Tess's duplicity. 'The picture of life had changed for him' (p. 332).

COMMENTARY

Angel's expectations about peasant girls are current in his family. Our narrator highlights the Clares' limitations. Angel Clare is conventionally hidebound, despite his supposed rejection of social custom and his own very sensuous memories of Tess. The moral of the novel is addressed and, with particular stress being placed on Tess's purity, a clear authorial position emerges: 'In considering what Tess was not,' we are told, 'he overlooked what she was, and forgot that the defective can be more than the entire' (p. 338).

> **GLOSSARY**
>
> 332   **Wiertz** the Wiertz Museum, Brussels, holds the work of Anton Wiertz (1806–65), who specialised in morbid subjects
>
> **Van Beers** Jan van Beers (1852–1927) was a Belgian painter of common everyday life
>
> **Pagan moralist** Roman emperor Marcus Aurelius (AD121–80)
>
> **'Let not your heart … be afraid'** Bible, John 14:27
>
> **the Nazarene** Jesus Christ
>
> 335   **a good thing could … Nazareth** Bible, John 1:46

> **CONTEXT**
>
> Cattle ranching was slower to take off in Brazil than in neighbouring Argentina or Uruguay due, among other factors, to less suitable soil, lack of sufficient railroads, a shortage of foreign investors and limited local capital. The industry did not therefore really take off until the late nineteenth century, and potential settlers had to be attracted via financial incentives such as cheap land and passage.

CHAPTER 40

- Angel banks thirty pounds for Tess.
- He leaves the country.

While he is sorting out his affairs Angel meets Miss Mercy Chant. He puts the jewels in the bank, deposits thirty pounds for Tess's use and writes to tell her what he has done; she is to contact his family if in need. He goes back to Wellbridge to settle up. While he is there Izz Huett appears, 'an honest girl who loved him – one who would have made as good, or nearly as good, a practical farmer's wife as Tess' (p. 341). He offers her a lift home, and on the way asks her to go to Brazil with him. She agrees, but when she says that no one could have loved him more than Tess, he abandons her. Five days later he leaves for Brazil.

COMMENTARY

Angel is tempted to fall into Alec's evil ways here; when deeply distressed he is morally inconsistent. Notice the sharp contrast between Izz Huett and Mercy Chant. Angel's attempt to take up with Izz Huett, a carbon copy of Tess, prefigures his relationship with Tess's younger sister in Chapter 59.

GLOSSARY		
339	a parlous state in a wretched condition, see Shakespeare, *As You Like It*, Act III Scene 2	
343	prophet on the top of Peor Balaam who prophesied and blessed the future of the Israelites: Bible, Numbers 22–4	

CHAPTER 41

- Tess is impoverished and must find work for the winter.
- Angel is reportedly ill.

Eight months later, Tess is impoverished. She has had to use her allowance to buy food, winter clothes and a new thatch for her parents' cottage. She does not want to ask for more money and sets out to join Marian, 'the good-natured and now tippling girl' (p. 349), on an upland farm. As she travels she is accosted by the man who insulted her in Chapter 33. She runs away and hides in a wood. During the night she hears wounded pheasants dying and falling from the trees. In the morning she kills them. Meanwhile, we are told that Clare is ill in Brazil.

COMMENTARY

Tess is like a wounded animal. As she hides in the wood she compares the birds' suffering to her own. The season as always reflects the mood of the narrative and Tess's progress through her short life. Moments of repetition across the novel such as Tess's meeting with the man who insulted her continue to add to its architectural structure.

GLOSSARY

348	*éclat* (French) brilliant success
349	Black Care Horace, *Odes*, III, 1
351	'All is vanity' Bible, Ecclesiastes 1:2

CHAPTER 42

- Tess reaches a remote farm, where she is taken on as a field hand.

Tess wards off further casual enquiries by dressing poorly and making herself look ugly. She tries to get other work, but finally arrives at Flintcomb-Ash, where she reluctantly signs on for the winter. Tess makes Marian swear not to tell anyone she is married.

COMMENTARY

The chapter begins by focusing on Tess's feelings and self-immolation, but draws back to reveal a new, barren landscape. Tess is still submissive in her suffering, almost as a matter of pride, as suggested in Chapter 38. The phrase 'Tess walks on; a figure which is part of the landscape; a fieldwoman pure and simple, in winter guise' (p. 355) is reminiscent of the description of women working the harvest field in Chapter 14. It, along with the rest of the description, is also evocative of a dramatic setting and stage direction.

QUESTION

To what extent does the landscape through which she passes and in which she works reflect Tess's social and moral standing?

> **GLOSSARY**
>
> | | |
> |---|---|
> | 354 | mommet (dialect) a scarecrow |
> | 355 | 'The maiden's mouth ... head' A. C. Swinburne, 'Fragoletta' |
> | | Cybele the Many-breasted Phrygian goddess of nature, often depicted with many breasts |
> | 356 | plashed down with the quickset woven and bent down to form a thick hedge |
> | 358 | starve-acre not fertile |
> | 359 | Old Lady-Day Feast of the Annunciation; 6 April in the old, pre-1752 calendar, now 25 March |

CHAPTER 43

- Tess's work is hard.
- She tries to write to Angel for help, but cannot finish her letter.

When Marian and Tess work in the fields they can just see Talbothays and this prompts them to talk about the past. Marian drinks and Tess still hopes that Angel will return. Izz Huett joins them as they work in the barn with Dark Car and her sister, the Queen of Diamonds. Their employer is the man who insulted Tess in Chapter 33. Izz tells Marian, who tells Tess, about Angel's proposition and Tess is stung to write to him, but she cannot finish the letter.

COMMENTARY

Hardy describes the women's field work in detail, but also likens the landscape to the human form. This **anthropomorphic** treatment suggests that Hardy is not simply concerned with the scrupulous representation of the women's employment or of human nature; things are not presented as they are, so the chapter is much less realist than it appears. The women are dehumanised by the work, 'their movements [showing] a mechanical regularity' (pp. 360–1), but their concerns and experiences are equally reduced by the

CONTEXT

Whereas working with poultry, in a dairy or in a harvest field were all deemed 'respectable' forms of employment for rural women, field work was not. Reports in the 1860s on women's and children's work in the fields argued that it was physically and morally corrupting.

immaterial, transcendental or **metaphysical** power of nature, as represented by the passage of nameless arctic birds, silent witnesses to grotesque, unimaginable horrors.

The return of minor characters serves to remind us of Tess's earlier relationship with Alec. Again, Tess is likened to Mary Magdalene, as she was in Chapter 20. Coincidences like this add to the overall sense of conspiracy.

CONTEXT

Hardy's descriptions of field work have often been likened to the semi-impressionist rural paintings of the artist George Clausen (1852–1944), who founded the New English Art Club in 1866.

GLOSSARY		
360	lanchets or lynchets	(dialect) beds of flint
	siliceous	quartz
361	the two Marys	the Virgin Mary, mother of Christ, and Mary Magdalene
363	Aurora	*Aurora borealis* is a spectacle of the Poles
	terraqueous	of earth and water
364	reed-drawing	preparing straw for thatching
366	Amazonian	Amazons are legendary warrior women
370	thirtover	(dialect) cross, contrary, stubborn

CHAPTER 44

- Tess finally decides to seek help from Angel's parents.
- On her way back from the empty vicarage, she sees Alec preaching.

Tess decides to see Angel's family, fifteen miles away. Marian and Izz help to dress her simply but prettily. It is noon when she arrives at Emminster. She changes her boots and goes down to the vicarage. Everyone is at church, and while waiting for Mr and Mrs Clare she overhears a conversation between Angel's brothers, who are taking a stroll before dinner. They are talking about Angel 'throwing himself away upon a dairymaid' (p. 376) as they pass her. Then, when they catch up with Mercy Chant, several derogatory remarks

CONTEXT

The poor in the nineteenth century were deemed to be either 'deserving' or 'undeserving' by those in a position to help them. The 1834 Poor Law Amendment Act was designed to ensure that no one would seek aid from a workhouse unless they had no other choice, and private charities were careful to select those they helped on the basis of good, moral behaviour. Begging, or vagrancy, was meant to be strictly controlled by law.

are made about Tess's boots, which they find in the hedge. Disheartened, Tess gives up and walks back to Flintcomb-Ash. On the way she stops to hear a preacher in a barn and is surprised to see that it is Alec d'Urberville.

COMMENTARY

The chapter brings the phase to an end by providing Tess with her last real chance of help from Angel, and by reintroducing Alec. The way she is dressed up by Marian and Izz mirrors the way her mother dressed her up in Chapter 7. Chapter 25 adds to the pathos of her failure. Notice the bloodied piece of paper that blows up and down outside the vicarage, also the painter of signs in Alec's congregation.

GLOSSARY

372	crape quilling closely pleated material
376	*guindée* (French) stiff, prim
378	Publicans and Sinners despised groups in the Bible, Mark 2:16
	Scribes and Pharisees religious leaders, Mark 2:16
379	ranter vehement preacher
	antinomian Antinomanism holds the view that Christians are released from the obligation of observing the moral law
	'O foolish Galatians ...' Bible, Galatians 3:1

 CHECK THE NET

For information about life and poverty in London, collected by Charles Booth from the late 1880s to 1890s, search **http:// booth.lse.ac.uk**

PHASE THE SIXTH – THE CONVERT

CHAPTER 45

- Alec makes Tess swear that she will never tempt him.

Tess is shocked at first, then quickly leaves the barn. Alec sees her, falters in his preaching and catches her up. He tells her that he was converted by the Reverend Mr Clare after Mrs d'Urberville died. Tess does not believe that Alec has changed, and compares him to Angel, who has rejected his father's faith. Just before leaving her Alec makes her swear, on what he thinks is a cross, that she will not tempt him. A shepherd tells Tess that the 'Cross-in-Hand … a strange rude monolith … on which was roughly carved a human hand' (p. 389) is really an ill-omened memorial.

COMMENTARY

The reader has trouble believing in Alec's conversion. He has apparently taken up elements of Angel in the way that Angel took on aspects of Alec in Chapter 40. He becomes Adam to her Eve; the suggestion is that he will fall to her temptation. There is irony in his relating the story of his earlier run-in with Mr Clare, and in his making Tess swear on an evil stone.

CHECK THE FILM

Alec is not represented in as much detail in Roman Polanski's 1979 film as in Hardy's novel, because Polanski had to communicate characteristics quickly via common visual cues. For example, Alec does not become a lay preacher in the film and he is portrayed quite stereotypically as a moustachioed 'baddie'.

GLOSSARY	
383	*bizarrerie* (French) strangeness
	Paulinism following St Paul's teaching
384	Cyprian image image of Venus, Roman goddess of love
385	Methodist originally followers of John Wesley (1703–91), who broke away from the Anglican Church
386	wrath to come Bible, Matthew 3:7
	'Come out … Lord' Bible, II Corinthians 6:17
391	wuld (dialect) old
	petite mort (French) faintness

CHAPTER 46

- Alec asks Tess to marry him.
- When he visits her at her cottage, she tests his faith.

Alec visits Tess while she is working and asks her to go with him to Africa as a missionary's wife. She tells him that she cannot marry

CONTEXT

Nineteenth-century novels set in Britain frequently make reference to the wider world, especially the British and other empires, in the same way as *Tess of the d'Urbervilles*. Britain was the centre of a vast, global network, and authors took references to Africa or to colonial culture and projects, such as missionary work, as givens.

and he gleans a little of her circumstances. When they are interrupted by the farmer Alec defends Tess from his insults. At the end of the day, she tries to write to Angel, but fails.

The others go to a hiring fair and Alec visits Tess while she is alone. They discuss Angel's doctrinal views and Alec tells her that by visiting her instead of preaching he has fallen.

COMMENTARY

The oddly theological discussion in the cottage holds Angel and Alec in tension. Tess is again likened to Eve and Alec blames her for his fall from grace. He appears to struggle with his conscience, but the use of irony – Alec is himself later characterised as 'ironic' (Chapter 51, p. 438) – is again strong. It is Angel's words that undo his father's conversion and make Alec lose his faith. There are also parallels between the two men in the idea of emigration, and in Alec's threatening Tess's employer. Both Angel and Alec contemplate taking Tess abroad.

GLOSSARY

396	'The unbelieving husband … husband' Bible, I Corinthians 7:14
398	Candlemas Fair 2 February
400	Sermon on the Mount Bible, Matthew 5–7
401	*Dictionnaire Philosophique* sceptical work by Voltaire (1764)
	Huxley's Essays *Essays upon some Controversial Questions* (1892), T. H. Huxley (1825–95), leading defence of Charles Darwin's (1809–82) theories; Huxley coined the word 'agnosticism'
	like the devils … tremble Bible, James 2:19
402	serve in the groves associated with the worship of Baal: Bible, II Kings 17–23
	'servants of corruption' Bible, II Peter 2:19–20
	witch of Babylon the whore of Babylon: Bible, Revelation 17

CHAPTER 47

- Alec, having lost his faith, turns up while Tess is threshing.
- Again he tries to persuade her to go with him.

It is March and the last wheat rick has to be threshed by a steam-driven threshing machine. The work is unremitting and Tess is chosen for one of the hardest tasks: untying the sheaves so that the corn can be fed into the hopper. Alec, who has now lost his faith and his morality, appears while they break for lunch and offers to take her away. She hits him with her glove and makes his lip bleed. He leaves, but promises to return.

COMMENTARY

The scene is set at a distance, in the present tense, the machine is given human qualities and made to seem alien through the use of complex language. Shifting into the past tense, the narration then focuses on the gathering labourers. The machine is a metaphor for Tess's life. It has also been read as a symbol of the agricultural revolution which has swept away the old relationships of the countryside, so that men like Alec, who do not care about or understand their obligations, now stand in the place of old feudal families such as the d'Urbervilles, who had a more organic relationship with the land and its people.

There are several links here to other chapters which help move the text on towards a conclusion. The monstrous threshing machine can be compared to the blood-red reaping machine in Chapter 14 and the train in Chapter 30. Finally, when she strikes Alec Tess gets a taste for his blood that is really only satisfied when she murders him in Chapter 57. But, despite the structure of repetitions, there is change in Tess's character, for example she 'had gathered from Angel sufficient of the incredulity of modern thought to despise flash enthusiasms' (pp. 408–9), and Alec comments that he has seen her change.

 CHECK THE BOOK

Merryn Williams's *Thomas Hardy and Rural England* (Macmillan, 1972) provides a classic analysis of Hardy's construction of the rural and social change, as encapsulated in the scene with the threshing machine. Williams argues that in Hardy's view, it is the farmer's intention of exploiting his workers to the utmost that is degrading, rather than the machine.

GLOSSARY

404	*primum mobile* (Latin) 'first mover', that which sets the world in motion
	Tophet a place where fire was kept burning: Bible, Isaiah 30:33
405	aborigines used in the Latin sense, 'those there from the beginning' (this does not appear in all editions)
	steam threshing-machine introduced in Britain in the 1840s, but not widely used until the second half of the nineteenth century
	Plutonic Pluto, Roman god of hell
	autochthonous native
407	nor the seven thunders Bible, Revelation 10:3–4 (this does not appear in all editions)
	hagrode (dialect) bewitched, tormented by nightmares
408	*Weltlust* (German) lust for life
409	Hymenaeus and Alexander Bible, I Timothy 1:19–20
	bachelor-apostle St Paul
	let go the plough Bible, Luke 9:62
411	words of … Hosea Bible, Hosea 2:7

? QUESTION

Hardy chose a rural idyll for his setting, the better to comment on the condition of his own time and place, especially the experience of modernity. Discuss.

CHAPTER 48

- At the end of the day, Alec returns and offers to help Tess's family.
- She is troubled enough to write to Angel for solace.

The threshing continues into the evening and Alec returns as promised. The rats that run out of the last sheaf are hunted down and the work finishes. Alec and Tess seem to make up. He offers to help her and her family, but again she refuses any aid. On returning to her cottage she writes to Angel and pleads for him to return.

COMMENTARY

The tension builds as Alec continues to pursue Tess, as if she were one of the rats which emerge at the end of the threshing. Tess is again likened to a wounded animal, this time a 'bled calf' (p. 415). Alec goes after her when she is at her weakest, and the offer to help her family, echoing his original offer of aid in Chapter 11, is aimed at her most vulnerable point.

It is interesting to see how fluid her letter to Angel is. In deep distress, she writes to him as a woman educated 'into the proportions of social things', not as 'an unapprehending peasant' (Chapter 35, p. 302). The letter presents one of the few occasions on which Tess is apparently given her own voice. Compare the escaping rats to the escaping animals in the harvest field in Chapter 14.

? QUESTION

How important is Tess's background in determining her actions and the ways in which others treat her?

GLOSSARY	
413	'nammet'-time (dialect) mid-morning or mid-afternoon break
414	Jacob's ladder Bible, Genesis 28:10–13
415	Pandemonium city of the devils in John Milton's *Paradise Lost*
418	my last state … my first Bible, Matthew 12:45, Luke 11:26

CHAPTER 49

- Angel is a changed man.
- Tess leaves Flintcomb-Ash to help her parents.

Tess's letter is sent on to Angel via the vicarage. Angel has been ill and, influenced by a stranger, now regrets his treatment of Tess. While away he has 'mentally aged a dozen years' (p. 421). Meanwhile, Tess waits for Angel's reply and practises singing the ballads he liked. Old Lady-Day is approaching, but, just before Tess's term is up, 'Liza-Lu appears and asks Tess to go to their mother and father. Tess leaves her sister to catch up the next day and sets off home.

COMMENTARY

The chapter focuses on Clare and it is possible to argue that he has been completely transformed by his experiences in Brazil; however, there are a number of subsequent events and images in the text that seem to contradict this reading, as we will see. The letter is used to take us first to the vicarage, where we are filled in on what has been happening in Brazil, and then on to Brazil itself.

'Liza-Lu is very much the image of the young 'inviolate' Tess – this becomes significant in Chapter 58. Fate continues to conspire against Tess – we hear that her parents are ill immediately after Alec has offered help.

GLOSSARY

420	as Abraham … hill together Abraham was told by God to sacrifice his son, Isaac: Bible, Genesis 22:1–13
422	Hellenic Paganism Greek philosophy
423	reasoning is somewhat musty Shakespeare, *Hamlet*, Act III Scene 2
424	gleaning of the grapes … Abi-ezer Bible, Judges 8:2
425	drave toil
426	withy basket basket made from plaited willow

CHAPTER 50

- Tess cares for her parents.
- Alec turns up again.
- She spurns him, but on her return home finds her father has died.

It is over a year since Tess has been home. She helps her mother to get well and sets about planting up the garden and allotment with her father. One evening, she finds Alec d'Urberville working beside her. Again, he offers to help her family and again she refuses his aid. When Tess returns to the house she finds that her father has died. Her family will therefore have to leave the cottage.

COMMENTARY

This is Tess's third and final return home, this time in darkness, seen through her own eyes. The world feels unreal, the landscape reflects her history which is mingled with its own, and her perceptions are changed just as they were when she went walking at night in Chapter 13. Alec's sudden reappearance by firelight, holding a pitchfork, reminds us of his devilish aspect, which is reinforced when he calls her Eve and names himself 'the old Other One' (p. 431). This is reminiscent of Chapter 45, in which Alec made Tess swear on a stone that commemorated a man who had sold his soul to the devil, but it also brings together the imagery of fire – for instance, her confession in Chapter 34 – and of the Fall – in which she has been figured both as Eve and the snake – which have dogged Tess throughout the novel. The pressure is building for Tess, who needs Alec's help as soon as she has refused it. The reference to a kind of natural justice in the family's removal from their cottage echoes that in Chapter 11 – the reference to eviction also reminds us of the cottage in which Tess worked in Chapter 9.

CONTEXT

Social reformers argued throughout the nineteenth century that agricultural labourers should be provided with some ground, e.g. a garden, allotment or 'potato ground', on which they could grow food. A similar argument was made about those who lived and worked in the towns. In 1887 the Allotment Act required authorities to supply allotments if there was a demand.

GLOSSARY	
427	turnpike-roads main roads, on which a toll was levied
	pricked and ducked suspected witches were tested by pinpricks and by ducking in water
	'whickered' (dialect) to neigh, to giggle
429	hired labour paid work for the farmer
	couch-grass persistent weed
430	'pillar of a cloud' God, as a pillar of cloud by day and fire by night, led the Israelites out of Egypt: Bible, Exodus 13:21
431	Other One the devil
	'Empress, the way … Eve John Milton, *Paradise Lost*, IX.626–31, where Satan tempts Eve

continued

CONTEXT

Most farmers in the nineteenth century were tenant farmers, in other words they rented their farms from landlords.

> 434 'liviers' life-tenants
> determined reached its end
> Olympians Olympus was the home of the classical gods

CHAPTER 51

- The Durbeyfields lose their home.
- Tess writes an angry note to Angel.

Tess's family have to leave, and as Old Lady-Day arrives all is in flux. Alec appears while Tess is alone in the cottage. She tells him they must move because she is not a 'proper woman' (p. 438); they have arranged lodgings in Kingsbere. He offers to give her and her family shelter in the garden-house where she worked at Trantridge. She turns him down again and he rides off. Tess suddenly feels angry at Clare for leaving her in this situation and posts him a short, angry note.

CONTEXT

There was a housing shortage in rural areas throughout the nineteenth century. Most cottages were 'tied', i.e. provided as part of a labourer's hiring agreement, and would therefore have to be given up as soon as the labourer changed jobs or lost work.

COMMENTARY

This chapter again combines social commentary on change in the countryside with more **metaphysical** mythic, in this case folkloric, elements. Tess's history is placed in its social context, so that we see the material consequences of an ostensible loss of purity given that 'the [Durbeyfield] household had not been shining examples either of temperance, soberness, or chastity' (p. 436). Tess blames herself for her family's misfortunes as she did when their horse died. When Alec relates the story of the d'Urberville coach, it works both as an omen within the narrative, and prefigures Tess's actions in the next phase. The 'man with the paint-pot' (p. 439) reappears: he symbolises both moral boundaries and their transgression. Again, Tess speaks through a letter, this time impassioned, but still well written. The children's Sunday-school song adds **pathos**

CHAPTER 52

- The family find that their lodgings have fallen through.
- Tess's friends write to Angel telling him to come home.

On the way to Kingsbere the Durbeyfields stop at an inn, where Tess exchanges news with Marian and Izz. Just before Tess and her family reach their lodgings, they are told that the arrangement has fallen through. The carter drops their furniture off at Kingsbere church and Tess's mother makes up a bed by the south wall, near the d'Urberville tomb. Tess is frightened by Alec, who rises from one of the tombs in the church and again offers to help her. Tess sends him away, but wishes that she were dead. In the meantime, Izz and Marian wonder if they can help Tess; a month later they write to Angel, who is on his way back to Britain.

COMMENTARY

The motif of the decayed family peaks in this faintly **gothic** chapter: 'Why', she asks herself as she leans on the entrance to the church vault, 'am I on the wrong side of this door!' (p. 449). Alec, who has assumed the d'Urberville name, springs from the family tomb. Izz and Marian's slightly archaic and ill-spelt letter – similar in style to Joan's letter in Chapter 31 – drives home the dangers that now surround Tess.

CONTEXT

See Hardy's poem 'The Ruined Maid' for a satirical take on the relative position of women who maintain their moral worth and those who don't.

GLOSSARY	
444	as the hexagon to the bee as honeycomb to the bee
	Ark of the Covenant religious symbol of the Israelites
445	superincumbent lying on top
	stale urinate
447	deparked no longer parkland of a great house (this does not appear in all editions)
448	brasses memorial plates in set stone
	Ostium sepulchri … d'Urberville door to d'Urberville tomb
449	The old order changeth Tennyson, 'Morte d'Arthur'
	tole (dialect) entice

PHASE THE SEVENTH – FULFILMENT

CHAPTER 53

- Angel returns and sets out to find Tess.

At Emminster, the Clare family are shocked by Angel's appearance when he finally returns: they 'could see the skeleton behind the man, and almost the ghost behind the skeleton' (p. 454). He has received Tess's plea for help and now he reads her rebuke. He hesitates to go to her because of this and writes to her instead. He gets a reply from Joan, who says Tess is away, she cannot say where. After rereading Tess's letters, and the one from Marian and Izz, Angel decides to find her.

COMMENTARY

This chapter leads us into the **denouement**. A sense of mystery and suspense is generated through Tess's absence – a detective plot becomes dominant for a while. Neither Clare nor the reader knows where she is or what has happened to her, but we are reminded of her feelings when he reads and rereads her letters.

GLOSSARY

454   the Word of God

       Crivelli's dead *Christus* fifteenth-century painting of crucified Christ

456   'which alters ... finds' Shakespeare, Sonnet 116

       Faustina wife of Marcus Aurelius (AD121–80), debauched

       Cornelia wife of Pompey (106–48BC), virtuous

       Lucretia innocent but raped by Tarquin (534–510BC)

       Phryne celebrated Greek courtesan (fourth century BC)

       the woman taken usually assumed to be Mary Magdalene: Bible, John 8:3–12

       wife of Uriah Bathsheba, who committed adultery with King David; he later arranged Uriah's death and married her

---

CHAPTER 54

- Angel follows Tess's trail.

Angel sets out to find Tess; he travels to Flintcomb-Ash, Marlott – where he pays for John Durbeyfield's headstone – and Kingsbere. Eventually he arrives at Joan's cottage. Joan is reluctant to tell him anything, but finally lets him know that Tess is at Sandbourne, a fashionable resort. Angel immediately catches the last train there.

COMMENTARY

As Clare retraces Tess's steps we are reminded of what has happened to her since he left her. Contrast his reactions to Tess's old home with his response to Talbothays' farmhouse in Chapter 25. His journey to and feelings about the Marlott cottage can be compared to Tess's in Chapter 50. His pursuit from Flintcomb-Ash is similar to Alec's. Sir John's headstone, 'HOW ARE THE MIGHTY FALLEN' (p. 460), fixes in stone what the parson says to him in Chapter 1.

CONTEXT

For a discussion of the religious values attached to Angel and Alec, see Ross C. Murfin, *Swinburne, Hardy, Lawrence and the Burden of Belief* (University of Chicago Press, 1978).

> **GLOSSARY**
>
> | 459 | a tale told by an idiot Shakespeare, *Macbeth*, Act V Scene 5 |
> | 460 | How are the Mighty Fallen Bible, II Samuel 1:19, 25 |

CHAPTER 55

- Angel meets Tess.
- She is staying in a lodging house with Alec.

Angel takes lodgings in Sandbourne, but asks himself, 'Where could Tess possibly be, a cottage-girl, his young wife, amidst all this wealth and fashion?' (p. 463). Having failed to find Tess the night before, he sets out early the next morning and gets her address from a postman. He finds her, considerably altered in dress and manner, staying at a lodging house under the name Mrs d'Urberville. She tells him that Alec helped her family and therefore managed to win her round. Convinced that she was really a deserted wife, she became tractable to Alec's wishes. She says that Angel's return has come too late and though she now hates Alec she insists that Angel leave.

COMMENTARY

The description of Sandbourne highlights how this is an utterly alien landscape for Tess. Alec's name goes unsaid, but he has fulfilled his promise to dress her 'with the best', as he said he would in Chapter 12 (p. 125). Her clothes heighten her 'natural beauty' like the jewels Angel gave her in Chapter 34. Finally mastered by Alec, Tess is no longer herself; her spirit and her body are sundered (compare to Chapters 18 and 35). The **pathos** of this painful chapter is also pointed up by the reference to Tess's 'fluty' voice (p. 466), the first thing about her that caught Angel's attention in Chapter 18, and by the softness of her hands, once reddened by dairy work.

CONTEXT

In the Victorian period it was assumed that a woman's clothes reflected not only her class and social position, but also her moral standing. Prostitutes were, for instance, said to typically dress in 'finery' – lace, feathers, satins and velvets – such finery suggesting that they were dressing above their station and, when tattered, connoting their moral impropriety.

> **GLOSSARY**
>
> | 463 | the prophet's gourd Bible, Jonah 4:10 |

CHAPTER 56

- The landlady overhears Tess and Alec arguing.
- Later, she sees a bloodstain on the ceiling.

Mrs Brooks, the landlady, 'not a person of an unusually curious turn of mind' (p. 468), follows Tess upstairs, listens at her door and looks through the keyhole. She overhears Tess's lament, but retreats in fear of being discovered. Later on, she sees Tess leave and, later still, looks up to see a growing red stain on the ceiling. She gets a workman to open the door and Alec is found dead in bed. The alarm is raised.

 CHECK THE FILM
'Drip, drip, drip' (p. 471). This is one of the most effective scenes in Roman Polanski's *Tess* (1979).

COMMENTARY

This chapter contains detail that is almost surgical – the knife just clips Alec's heart – and reads like a court testimony. This detachment, coupled with Mrs Brooks's **point of view**, generates a sense of suspense.

GLOSSARY

468	Ixionian wheel	in classical myth, Ixion was punished by being fastened to an eternally revolving wheel in hell
471	wafer	small piece of sealing-wax

CHAPTER 57

- Tess finds Angel and tells him she has murdered Alec.
- After wandering northward for some time, they hide in an empty house.

On checking out of his hotel, Angel receives a message that one of his brothers has got engaged to Mercy Chant. Angel goes to the railway station, but, tired of waiting, decides to walk on to the next.

Tess catches him up and tells him that she has murdered Alec in order to be free again. Angel is not sure if this is actually the case, but decides to protect her. Dazed, they walk on into the countryside and find shelter in a deserted house.

COMMENTARY

There are elements of the sensational as well as of tragedy in this chapter, which ties up several loose ends and plot points prefigured in earlier passages. Tess hit Alec with her gauntlet in Chapter 47, thus, by her own admission, foreshadowing the murder. Angel can love Tess now that Alec is dead, as he said he might in Chapter 36. Tess says she killed Alec after he called Angel 'a foul name' (p. 475) – Angel hit Farmer Groby for a similar offence to Tess in Chapter 33. Atalanta is first mentioned in Chapter 25, again in Chapter 35, both times from her point of view. Notice too the return of the d'Urberville coach and further reference to the depravities or madness of the decayed d'Urberville blood that contaminates Tess's veins.

Though Angel and Tess wander reborn like babes in the wood – Tess is 'at last content', while tenderness is 'absolutely dominant in Clare at last' (p. 475) – the reader is never allowed to forget that their idyll is haunted by 'a corpse'.

GLOSSARY		
475	Antinous	beautiful youth beloved of the Emperor Hadrian
	Apollo	classical sun god; a type of beauty
478	Atalanta	huntress who is averse to marriage; she will not marry anyone who cannot beat her in a race; in some versions she spears the losers

CHECK THE FILM
Compare the way in which Polanski and Hardy use the savage, pagan imagery of Stonehenge, and the extent to which Hardy may come across as the more atheistic.

CHAPTER 58

- After a week in the house, Tess and Angel are discovered.
- They reach Stonehenge, where the police finally surround them.

Tess and Angel stay in the empty house for about a week, protected by a dense fog. Finally someone comes to air it and sees them sleeping. They wake and flee northward; passing through Melchester at midnight they finally come across Stonehenge in the darkness. Tess is tired and they rest. She asks him to marry 'Liza-Lu, who 'has all the best of me [Tess] without the bad' (p. 485). Angel is unable to say that they will meet in heaven. As Tess sleeps the police arrive; they arrest her when she wakes.

COMMENTARY

In this chapter there is considerable narrative play between rapid movement across great tracts of land, and stillness, while Tess and Angel hide, and quite complex yet **naturalised** dialogue, which provides Tess with her last chance to speak. The strangeness of the landscape is produced by drawing on both Angel's and Tess's points of view.

The sun has been a significant motif throughout the novel and here Tess is sacrificed in an ancient temple dedicated to the sun. In this chapter Angel kisses Tess as she lies on an ancient altar-stone, which echoes Chapter 37 in which he laid her in an abbot's coffin, and we may wonder whether he has changed at all. However, Tess does manage to teach Angel to live for the pleasure of the present, 'of now' (p. 480), which she tried but failed to do during their engagement.

 QUESTION

Where else is Tess associated with the sun, and what might this association connote?

> **GLOSSARY**
>
> 486   **Like a greater than himself** like Jesus, who remained silent before his accusers; Bible, Matthew 26:62–3, 27:12–14, and John 19:9–10

CHAPTER 59

• Angel and 'Liza-Lu watch from afar as the black flag that
  signals a hanging is raised over Wintoncester prison.

It is July. Angel and 'Liza-Lu are walking up a hill out of
Wintoncester in the early morning. They stop beside a milestone as
the clock strikes eight and watch the prison which they have just
left. They see a black flag raised, they appear to pray, then move on.

COMMENTARY

The final chapter is narrated at a distance, with complete
detachment. Tess's execution is placed within the context of the fate
that marked her at the outset of the novel and with reference to the
tombs of the d'Urbervilles. 'Liza-Lu is constructed as an innocent
version and 'a spiritualized image' (p. 488) of Tess, in other words,
as the idealised woman Angel loved all along.

EXTENDED COMMENTARIES

TEXT 1 – CHAPTER 4 (PP. 70–2)

Left to his reflections Abraham soon grew drowsy. Tess was not
skilful in the management of a horse, but she thought that she
could take upon herself the entire conduct of the load for the
present, and allow Abraham to go to sleep if he wished to do so.
She made him a sort of nest in front of the hives, in such a
manner that he could not fall, and, taking the reins into her own
hands, jogged on as before.

Prince required but slight attention, lacking energy for
superfluous movements of any sort. With no longer a companion
to distract her, Tess fell more deeply into reverie than ever, her
back leaning against the hives. The mute procession past her
shoulders of trees and hedges became attached to fantastic scenes
outside reality, and the occasional heave of the wind became the
sigh of some immense sad soul, conterminous with the universe
in space, and with history in time.

Then, examining the mesh of events in her own life, she seemed to see the vanity of her father's pride; the gentlemanly suitor awaiting herself in her mother's fancy; to see him as a grimacing personage, laughing at her poverty, and her shrouded knightly ancestry. Everything grew more and more extravagant, and she no longer knew how time passed. A sudden jerk shook her in her seat, and Tess awoke from the sleep into which she, too, had fallen.

They were a long way further on than when she had lost consciousness, and the waggon had stopped. A hollow groan, unlike anything she had ever heard in her life, came from the front, followed by a shout of 'Hoi there!'

The lantern hanging at her waggon had gone out, but another was shining in her face – much brighter than her own had been. Something terrible had happened. The harness was entangled with an object which blocked the way.

In consternation Tess jumped down, and discovered the dreadful truth. The groan had proceeded from her father's poor horse Prince. The morning mailcart, with its two noiseless wheels, speeding along these lanes like an arrow, as it always did, had driven into her slow and unlighted equipage. The pointed shaft of the cart had entered the breast of the unhappy Prince like a sword, and from the wound his life's blood was spouting in a stream, and falling with a hiss into the road.

In her despair Tess sprang forward and put her hand upon the hole, with the only result that she became splashed from face to skirt with the crimson drops. Then she stood helplessly looking on. Prince also stood firm and motionless as long as he could; till he suddenly sank down in a heap.

By this time the mail-cart man had joined her, and began dragging and unharnessing the hot form of Prince. But he was already dead, and, seeing that nothing more could be done immediately, the mail-cart man returned to his own animal, which was uninjured.

'You was on the wrong side,' he said. 'I am bound to go on with the mail-bags, so that the best thing for you to do is to bide here with your load. I'll send somebody to help you as soon as I can. It is getting daylight, and you have nothing to fear.'

> **? QUESTION**
>
> Tess is often associated with images of blood. What connotations does blood acquire through the course of the novel?

He mounted and sped on his way; while Tess stood and waited. The atmosphere turned pale, the birds shook themselves in the hedges, arose, and twittered; the lane showed all its white features, and Tess showed hers, still whiter. The huge pool of blood in front of her was already assuming the iridescence of coagulation; and when the sun rose a hundred prismatic hues were reflected from it. Prince lay alongside still and stark; his eyes half open, the hole in his chest looking scarcely large enough to have let out all that had animated him.

''Tis all my doing – all mine!' the girl cried, gazing at the spectacle. 'No excuse for me – none. What will mother and father live on now? Aby, Aby!' She shook the child, who had slept soundly through the whole disaster. 'We can't go on with our load – Prince is killed!'

? QUESTION

Consider the issues facing a director adapting a novel like *Tess of the d'Urbervilles* for film.

This passage comes early on in *Tess of the d'Urbervilles* and is a turning point in the novel. Tess Durbeyfield and her younger brother Abraham have set out late at night to take some beehives to market for their father, Jack, who is too drunk to get up and drive the cart himself. He has been celebrating the discovery that he is a descendant of the ancient and aristocratic d'Urbervilles. Later on, because Tess feels responsible for the accident, she seeks help from a Mrs d'Urberville, whom her family wrongly suppose to be a distant relative. Just before the passage begins, Tess and Abraham have been discussing their fate, the feeling that they have been born in a 'blighted' world, and its largely pessimistic tone is framed by the rhetorical question that Abraham raises just before their horse is killed: 'How would it have been if we had pitched on a sound one?' (p. 70).

As Tess slips into her reverie her sleepiness is reflected in the commonplace sensation that the trees and hedges are processing past her as the horse and cart jog on through the night. But, as she drifts off, she enters a heightened state of awareness in which she seems to be drawn outside herself. While she dozes, Tess glimpses the future in which both of her gentlemanly suitors will scorn her 'shrouded knightly ancestry' (p. 70). This is an experience which she readily describes in Chapter 18 as the soul leaving the body, and is suggested here by the transformation of the landscape, which becomes ever more fantastical.

The spiritual state into which Tess enters is then contrasted with the all too physical world into which she wakes. We see the world from her **point of view** as she carefully settles Abraham down to sleep and begins to muse over her father's pride, her mother's ambition. This is why we are as ignorant as she of the accident; we have, in a sense, dozed off with her. Hardy successfully creates a feeling of someone suddenly waking up in confusion by describing what she sees and hears, rather than what has happened. In this way we feel Tess's horror and can better understand why she feels that she has let the horse be killed.

The death of the horse is obviously a financial calamity for the Durbeyfields, as Tess realises, and this simple economic fact leads her into the clutches of the deathly figure she has dreamed about: Alec d'Urberville. But it is also an omen. The passage is graphic and brutal; we see Tess peacefully falling asleep on the dark road, suddenly awakened by utter disaster for her and her family and powerless to stem the tide of Prince's lifeblood. The passage clearly prefigures that in Chapter 11 when she falls asleep and is penetrated by Alec d'Urberville. She will lose her innocence, stand for as long as she can, then fall, just like Prince. This effect is made clearer by the play of red on white in which Tess, whiter still than her surroundings, has been tinctured by blood.

The language at this point is deliberately scientific. In juxtaposition to the pragmatism of the mail-cart man, and with the waking birds, the prismatic play of sunlight suggests the total indifference of nature to Tess's troubles. The narrative moves from a distanced authorial comment, in which the narrator uses very abstract and Latinate words and phrases, to a more immediate dramatisation of the scene at hand, then back towards a remoter stance again as the scene closes.

TEXT 2 – CHAPTER 30 (PP. 250–2)

They crept along towards a point in the expanse of shade just at hand at which a feeble light was beginning to assert its presence, a spot where, by day, a fitful white streak of steam at intervals upon the dark green background denoted intermittent moments

CHECK THE FILM

Both Roman Polanski and Thomas Hardy hoped to create a sense of an almost eternal land, one that would outlive its human actors regardless of change.

of contact between their secluded world and modern life. Modern life stretched out its steam feeler to this point three or four times a day, touched the native existences, and quickly withdrew its feeler again, as if what it touched had been uncongenial.

They reached the feeble light, which came from the smoky lamp of a little railway station; a poor enough terrestrial star, yet in one sense of more importance to Talbothays Dairy and mankind than the celestial ones to which it stood in such humiliating contrast. The cans of new milk were unladen in the rain, Tess getting a little shelter from a neighbouring holly tree.

Then there was the hissing of a train, which drew up almost silently upon the wet rails, and the milk was rapidly swung can by can into the truck. The light of the engine flashed for a second upon Tess Durbeyfield's figure, motionless under the great holly tree. No object could have looked more foreign to the gleaming cranks and wheels than this unsophisticated girl, with the round bare arms, the rainy face and hair, the suspended attitude of a friendly leopard at pause, the print gown of no date or fashion, and the cotton bonnet drooping on her brow.

She mounted again beside her lover, with a mute obedience characteristic of impassioned natures at times, and when they had wrapped themselves up over head and ears in the sail-cloth again, they plunged back into the now thick night. Tess was so receptive that the few minutes of contact with the whirl of material progress lingered in her thought.

'Londoners will drink it at their breakfast to-morrow, won't they?' she asked. 'Strange people that we have never seen.'

'Yes – I suppose they will. Though not as we send it. When its strength has been lowered, so that it may not get up into their heads.'

'Noble men and noble women, ambassadors and centurions, ladies and tradeswomen, and babies who have never seen a cow.'

'Well, yes; perhaps; particularly centurions.'

'Who don't know anything of us, and where it comes from; or think how we two drove miles across the moor to-night in the rain that it might reach 'em in time?'

www. CHECK THE NET

To hear an interview with Roman Polanski, find the BBC Four Audio Interviews on the BBC website at **http://www.bbc. co.uk**

'We did not drive entirely on account of these precious Londoners; we drove a little on our own – on account of that anxious matter which you will, I am sure, set at rest, dear Tess. Now, permit me to put it in this way. You belong to me already, you know; your heart, I mean. Does it not?'

'You know as well as I. O yes – yes!'

'Then, if your heart does, why not your hand?'

'My only reason was on account of you – on account of a question. I have something to tell you –'

'But suppose it to be entirely for my happiness, and my worldly convenience also?'

'O yes; if it is for your happiness and worldly convenience. But my life before I came here – I want –'

'Well, it is for my convenience as well as my happiness. If I have a very large farm, either English or colonial, you will be invaluable as a wife to me; better than a woman out of the largest mansion in the country. So please – please, dear Tessy, disabuse your mind of the feeling that you will stand in my way.'

'But my history. I want you to know it – you must let me tell you – you will not like me so well!'

'Tell it if you wish to, dearest. This precious history then. Yes, I was born at so and so, Anno Domini –'

This passage comes almost midway through *Tess of the d'Urbervilles*. It is late summer and Tess Durbeyfield has been working for some time at Talbothays Dairy. Since she has been working there she has fallen in love with Angel Clare. He is the son of a parson, but, having fallen out with his father, hopes to become a farmer. Just before this passage begins, Angel Clare has offered to take the milk to the station with Tess in order to seek her hand. He has already proposed to her, but she has resisted his blandishments because she does not feel worthy of him. She has already been involved with another man, Alec d'Urberville. Angel will desert her on their wedding night when she finally confesses.

The passage is initially characterised by a description of Tess and Angel's journey to the station, in which Hardy shows the

> **? QUESTION**
>
> There is a sense of visual distance in much of Hardy's writing, a distance of the narrator from the action that creates a sense of **pathos**. To what extent might Hardy's writing therefore be described as cinematic?

dependence of the countryside upon urban markets and modern technology. It is in passages like this that we can see the degree to which Hardy is preoccupied with the modern. The strangeness of 'modern life' is suggested in the **metaphor** of a 'feeler' stretching out across the countryside (p. 251). Tess is captured and put on display by the light of the steam engine as if she were a scientific specimen. The modern world does not perceive Tess as a personality, she is simply one of the 'native existences' it finds 'uncongenial'. Tess is deeply affected by the experience, as we learn from the simple conversation that takes place when she and Angel move off again. She is visually reduced to the basest, most vulnerable, physical level by the train, but remains 'receptive' to what it represents.

The language in the passage shifts between a distanced, abstract narration which uses words like 'feelers' in reference to a simple railway track, and a more immediate narration of the thoughts and feelings of Tess and Clare, from their **point of view**. Tess is not so articulate as Clare, his education shows through in his confident use of language and contrasts sharply with her own clumsy attempt to express what she is thinking. She handles history badly, mixing 'centurions' (p. 251) in with nobles, even though she has been picking up 'his vocabulary, his accent, and fragments of his knowledge' (Chapter 28, p. 238). Angel teases her for this, but Tess resists Clare when he offers to teach her about history, because it is 'best … not to remember that your nature and your past doings have been just like thousands' and thousands', and that your coming life and doings'll be like thousands' and thousands'' (Chapter 19, p. 182). In this respect Tess rebels against the determinism that shapes her life and expresses the 'ache of modernism' (Chapter 19, p. 180) that Angel cannot understand.

Tess is represented here as modest and unassuming, but, as she stands like 'a friendly leopard at pause' (p. 251), we understand something of her underlying passion and complexity. Angel does not see her animal, 'impassioned' nature, however, only his 'unsophisticated girl'. Because of this rather one-sided view of her, he cannot believe that her 'history' might be a serious impediment to their marriage and he makes fun of her attempt to tell it. Later on

CHECK THE BOOK

Kevin Moore looks at Hardy's (often **ironic**) use of other writers, especially the English Romantics, in *The Descent of the Imagination: Post-Romantic Culture in the Later Novels of Thomas Hardy* (New York University Press, 1990).

in the novel, in Chapter 35, he remembers that he prevented her from confessing, but by that point no longer sees her as the woman whom he is in love with in this passage, his innocent and child-like 'Tessy'. The dialogue is broken up as he constantly cuts in on her. He is fixed in his determination to pursue his own argument to its logical conclusion and he makes it clear that he will brook no refusal; she will not stand in his way. Angel is a character who cannot alter his mind once it is made up; he is quite unbending and often seems to be just as coercive as the villainous Alec d'Urberville.

Text 3 – Chapter 59 (pp. 488–90)

One of the pair was Angel Clare, the other a tall budding creature – half girl, half woman – a spiritualized image of Tess, slighter than she, but with the same beautiful eyes – Clare's sister-in-law, 'Liza-Lu. Their pale faces seemed to have shrunk to half their natural size. They moved on hand in hand, and never spoke a word, the drooping of their heads being that of Giotto's 'Two Apostles'.

When they had nearly reached the top of the great West Hill the clocks in the town struck eight. Each gave a start at the notes, and, walking onward yet a few steps, they reached the first milestone, standing whitely on the green margin of the grass, and backed by the down, which here was open to the road. They entered upon the turf, and, impelled by a force that seemed to overrule their will, suddenly stood still, turned, and waited in paralyzed suspense beside the stone.

The prospect from this summit was almost unlimited. In the valley beneath lay the city they had just left, its more prominent buildings showing as in an isometric drawing – among them the broad cathedral tower, with its Norman windows and immense length of aisle and nave, the spires of St Thomas's, the pinnacled tower of the College, and, more to the right, the tower and gables of the ancient hospice, where to this day the pilgrim may receive his dole of bread and ale. Behind the city swept the rotund upland of St Catherine's Hill; further off, landscape beyond landscape, till the horizon was lost in the radiance of the sun hanging over it.

Against these far stretches of country rose, in front of the other city edifices, a large red-brick building, with level gray roofs, and

> **CONTEXT**
>
> The Romantics rejected the limitations of form and precedent and saw themselves as individuals who could express themselves according to their imagination. They explored everything that was felt to be mysterious, remote and unnerving, and assumed the mantle of prophets and legislators; the poet became a special kind of person, set apart from other people because of them. They saw nature as unmodified by humanity, inherently dazzling and elevating, and believed humanity should learn from nature personified as 'Nature'.

rows of short barred windows bespeaking captivity, the whole contrasting greatly by its formalism with the quaint irregularities of the Gothic erections. It was somewhat disguised from the road in passing it by yews and evergreen oaks, but it was visible enough up here. The wicket from which the pair had lately emerged was in the wall of this structure. From the middle of the building an ugly flat-topped octagonal tower ascended against the east horizon, and viewed from this spot, on its shady side and against the light, it seemed the one blot on the city's beauty. Yet it was with this blot, and not with the beauty, that the two gazers were concerned.

Upon the cornice of the tower a tall staff was fixed. Their eyes were riveted on it. A few minutes after the hour had struck something moved slowly up the staff, and extended itself upon the breeze. It was a black flag.

'Justice' was done, and the President of the Immortals, in Aeschylean phrase, had ended his sport with Tess. And the d'Urberville knights and dames slept on in their tombs unknowing. The two speechless gazers bent themselves down to the earth, as if in prayer, and remained thus a long time, absolutely motionless: the flag continued to wave silently. As soon as they had strength they arose, joined hands again, and went on.

This passage belongs to the final chapter of *Tess of the d'Urbervilles*. By this point Angel, who initially deserted Tess because of her affair with Alec d'Urberville, has learned to forgive her. While Angel is abroad, Tess has to support herself by working in the fields at Flintcomb-Ash. During this period she attempts to get help from Angel's family, and on her return runs into Alec, who claims to be converted. He soon loses his faith and begins to pursue her again. When her father dies, convinced that Angel will never come back, she consents to live with Alec. When Angel finds her living with him she is devastated; she kills Alec and runs after Angel. They hide, but after sharing a few brief days of happiness, Tess is finally arrested at Stonehenge.

The novel ends in movement, as it began; Angel and 'Liza-Lu move mechanically like Tess's father did in his drunken journey home

CHECK THE BOOK

In *The Fabrication of the Late Victorian Femme Fatale* (Macmillan, 1992) Rebecca Stott notes that Tess is often described as fatally, sexually alluring, but argues that Tess is far more than just a victim. It is important to recognise the contradictions in Hardy's depiction of Tess.

from market in Chapter 1. The whole scene is written with detachment, so that we know nothing of Angel's and 'Liza-Lu's feelings as they watch 'Justice' being done; they do not speak, or think, they just act. As with the scene on The Chase, we do not see the actual violence committed against Tess, which is when her blood is, in a sense, first spilled, but we do overhear a degree of **ironical** authorial intervention. The indifference of 'the d'Urberville knights and dames' continues (p. 489). It is as if Tess had never lived.

We see images that have been closely associated with Tess throughout the novel – the prison is built of 'red-brick', the midsummer sun shines brightly – but she is represented by a new sign, 'a black flag'. Tess is brought to a standstill while her husband and her sister, who has her 'beautiful eyes', walk on. Much of the description is indeterminate, for instance Angel and 'Liza-Lu kneel '*as if* in prayer [my italics]', while the infinite spread of 'landscape beyond landscape' is dizzying. The sentences are long, but straightforward, adding to the impression of a long view. Here Hardy slips into a tourist-book style with a touch of Latinism in which he draws on his architectural training to describe Wintoncester's buildings, 'as in an isometric drawing' (p. 489).

We do not know if Angel and 'Liza-Lu marry, of course, but the fact that they walk off hand in hand suggests that they do. So, though this is the final chapter of the book and the theme of fate, or the inevitability of history, seems to conclude in the phrase 'the President of the Immortals … had ended his sport with Tess', this new relationship, described in the present tense, resists completeness and finality, or **closure**, in the text. The heroine is absent; what we actually see is 'Liza-Lu stepping into her place as 'a spiritualized image of Tess', ready to repeat the ancient history of the d'Urbervilles.

CHECK THE BOOK
See Rosemarie Morgan, *Women and Sexuality in the Novels of Thomas Hardy* (Routledge, 1988), for a valuable discussion of the extent to which Tess can be characterised as a 'passive' victim.

PART THREE

CRITICAL APPROACHES

CHARACTERISATION

Tess of the d'Urbervilles is like a medieval morality play, a **psychomachea,** in which Angel and Alec – the former representing virtue and the latter vice – seem to fight for the soul of Tess. Our understanding of each of the characters therefore depends, in part, on their relationship to the others in the novel.

TESS

CHECK THE FILM

Look at the way in which Tess is dressed in Roman Polanski's 1979 film: at the start she is in a simple cotton dress, by the end she is in a sophisticated gown and wearing a fashionable hat and veil. Compare this with the way in which Hardy represents Tess's transformation over the course of the novel.

Tess originally presented a problem for critics because of her 'purity'; today, it is still all too easy to ask, 'Do you support her?', to see her as a real person who is independent of the text. Tess of the d'Urbervilles, a pure woman, is, however, a complex fictional character who is used by Hardy to represent the insoluble social and biological ills of his day. Because of this complexity it is possible to read her, and therefore the novel, in a variety of ways.

First of all it is important to realise that Tess is a figure in whom oppositions like virgin and whore collapse; she is not one thing or the other, but both. Both unapprehending peasant and educated woman, she speaks two languages – the dialect of her home and an educated Sixth Standard English; she acts according to nature, but is sensitive to social convention; the passive innocent, she is still, in part, prideful and responsible for what happens to her; a victim, she is also a murderess. You cannot tell what she is just by looking at her, and the novel is structured around the dangers of misreading her as Angel and Alec do.

Tess initially belongs to the working class, then marries above her station. This representation of social mobility is part of the modern condition and reflects the period in which the novel was written. Because Tess is a modern rather than a Victorian character we, as modern readers, can identify with her. We find the novel painful because she feels the 'ache of modernism' (Chapter 19, p. 180), is impotent and inconsequential, and is the plaything of the 'President of the Immortals' (Chapter 59, p. 489).

Our eye is always drawn to Tess. Among the other binders she is 'the most flexuous and finely-drawn figure of them all' (Chapter 14, p. 138); it is her work which is described in detail, her arm whose 'feminine smoothness becomes scarified by the stubble, and bleeds' (Chapter 14, p. 138). Angel is apparently wrong to idealise Tess, yet the text itself sets her above the other women of her class. We are asked to note that 'The cheeks are paler, the teeth more regular, the red lips thinner than is usual in a country-bred girl' (Chapter 14, p. 138). And, in moments of emotional intensity, she seems to move beyond the bounds of ordinary, everyday life.

Tess is not always elevated; she is also represented as belonging to base nature. We are often given the impression that she communes with the animal kingdom and on these occasions she seems to be more animal than human. Tess is sympathetic to the wounded pheasants in Chapter 41; she is likened to 'a bled calf' in Chapter 48 (p. 415); as her captors catch up to her at Stonehenge, 'her breathing now was quick and small, like that of a lesser creature than a woman' (Chapter 58, p. 487). Her animality is used to make her appear vulnerable, but also to highlight her sexuality.

Hardy did not condemn Tess for her baser animal instincts, or for having had an illegitimate child, of course; she remained 'a pure woman' in his view, as the subtitle to the novel says. The problem for contemporary critics was that purity equated with virginity. When Tess is suddenly pitched from the pedestal of natural beauty into the mire of sexuality in The Chase, Hardy shows how women are wronged by the standards of his day. She was the exception that Hardy created to prove the rule. A heterogeneous figure, her society could not really understand or forgive a woman who was neither virgin nor whore, but contained aspects of both.

ALEC AND ANGEL

Alec and Angel pull Tess apart. Both are wilful, controlling, and guilty of harming Tess. The over-spiritualised Angel is more developed than the rather too-devilish Alec, but neither is easily

CHECK THE BOOK
When we first meet Tess, 'Phases of her childhood lurked in her aspect still' (Chapter 2, p. 52). For an interesting exploration of this element of her characterisation, see James R. Kincaid, *Child-Loving: The Erotic Child and Victorian Culture* (Routledge, 1992).

read as convincing or credible. They, in contrast to Tess, are more schematic, one-dimensional characters.

Angel and Alec are played off against each other and we are rarely surprised by their behaviour: Angel plays a harp, Alec appears as 'the old Other One' (Chapter 50, p. 431); the former is a physical Apollo, the latter has 'an almost swarthy complexion, with full lips … above which was a well-groomed black moustache with curled points' (Chapter 5, p. 79). Their physical appearance tells us everything about what they are like as men. Where Angel's love is spiritual, Alec's is material.

**CHECK
THE BOOK**

Marjorie Garson's
*Hardy's Fables of
Integrity: Woman,
Body, Text*
(Clarendon Press,
1991) carries a
useful analysis and
diagrammatic
representation of
Tess's relationship
with Alec and
Angel, and of each
man's relationship
to the other.

Sometimes, Alec and Angel echo each other's actions. The two men are not always unalike, and this helps prevent the novel from collapsing into two halves. For example, Angel momentarily takes on aspects of Alec's personality when he asks Izz to go with him to Brazil; both men think of taking Tess abroad; Alec loses his new-found faith thanks to Angel's ideas; both dress Tess up and try to make her into their own image; Angel sleepwalks with Tess to the abbot's tomb at Wellbridge, Alec rises from the tomb of the d'Urbervilles at Kingsbere.

Angel is a man of the 1890s who rejects the precepts of Christianity, as we learn in Chapter 18; an intellectual who is more logical than sensual, he falls prey to his emotions. He looks at Tess as a thing of beauty, he **objectifies** and idealises her, mistaking her for a goddess; he does not love her, as she says, for her *self*. He is the more complex of the two men in Tess's life, however, because he has the more complicated role. It is this character who helps us to fall in love with Tess, yet, representing the double standards of his day, then pulls away from her and rejects her utterly. It is easy to read him as a hypocrite at this point – given his own previous dalliance – but he does seem sensitive to the parallels in their experiences and finally, in part taking this on board, he returns to her, to show the reader how Tess has been wronged by the social conventions of his day.

Hardy extensively revised this character, during which process Angel's love became less sensual and more sensuous, and this rethinking made Angel's actions more consistent. When he falls out of love with Tess it is because she runs aground on 'a hard logical deposit' (Chapter 36, p. 311) which has always been there under the surface of his affection and because he has never loved her for herself, not because he is blind to her argument that 'I have forgiven you for the same!' (Chapter 35, p. 298). Today, however, Angel is not a sympathetic character, especially in the second half of the book, and his motivations are particularly difficult for the modern reader to understand.

Alec is little more than a cardboard cut-out. He is the more passionate lover and deals with Tess erotically from their first meeting when he asks, 'Well, my Beauty, what can I do for you?' (Chapter 5, p. 79). He rejects the old-fashioned moral standards and social conventions of his day and expects to master Tess as he does his horse. A cad and a bounder, he is selfish, arrogant, violent, capricious and superficial. But he is capable of slow seduction as well as domination, and this quality, coupled with his roguish good looks, can help us to understand how Tess becomes beguiled by him. Alec also knows that he is a bad man, but can do little about it. Despite his attempted conversion he remains in league with the devil. A real moustache-twirling villain from **melodrama**, he is quite hard for the reader to believe in. But his failed conversion does help to demonstrate the deterioration of Christianity in the modern world, and makes the character more interesting.

CHECK THE BOOK
For a reading of Alec that places him within the British **gothic** tradition, see Toni Reed, *Demon-Lovers and Their Victims in British Fiction* (University Press of Kentucky, 1988).

Alec and Angel are commonplace characters who are not really cut out to deal with or comprehend Tess's complexity, and neither character seems to go through any fundamental development. Alec's conversion – which became less and less sincere in each new version of the text – fails on all counts. A man of emotion rather than intellect, he cannot differentiate between faith and morality. Though Angel returns from Brazil to consummate his marriage, he still ultimately takes 'Liza-Lu, who is an idealised version of Tess, 'another woman in her shape', in her sister's place.

SECONDARY AND MINOR CHARACTERS

Tess's family are poor, but this is mostly because her parents are idle spendthrifts, not because they are 'peasants', as is made clear in Chapter 5. Tess's parents are proud and ambitious but profligate.

CHECK THE BOOK

For a basic discussion of some of the illustrations that appeared in the original serialised editions of Hardy's novels, see A.M. Jackson, *Illustration and the Novels of Thomas Hardy* (Rowman and Littlefield, 1981).

Tess's father is a tranter or small dealer; her mother cares for Tess, 'Liza-Lu, Abraham, Hope, Modesty, 'a boy of three' (Chapter 3, p. 61) and the baby. Tess has aspects of her mother and her father in her, and her family helps us to understand her character more thoroughly. Through them it is also made clear that Tess sees herself as the only industrious and dependable member of the household, and we are shown how Tess comes to take on responsibility for them, which shapes most of her decision-making.

Tess's mother has been seen by some critics as conspiring against her daughter, as setting her up in the hopes of acquiring social, or at least financial, advancement. She is not really a sympathetic character, but it is probably just as reasonable to lay the blame for Tess's downfall on Jack Durbeyfield. Jack is a drunkard. The novel opens with him staggering home from market, and it is his drinking that requires Tess to take the horse out on the fateful night it is killed. His feckless ways and large family leave the Durbeyfields in constant need.

Angel's family is not so well defined as Tess's, but there are still several chapters devoted to them. Angel's brothers, 'starched and ironed' (Chapter 44, p. 377), are introduced in Chapter 2, when Angel stops to dance with the village girls at the club-walking. When Angel first visits the vicarage in Emminster, in Chapter 25, we are introduced to his family at breakfast – including his absent elder sister via a portrait – all of them are, in some way or another, involved with the Church. From this chapter we gather that his father is supposed to be admirable and sincere; a staunch Evangelical, his precise sympathies are made known to us through his choice of quotations and his favourite theologians. All the family evince some difficulty in dealing with or understanding the lower classes, but it is evident from the outset that Angel's brothers are particularly bound by convention in this respect. Angel's parents are more generous than his brothers, as we are told in Chapters 39, 44 and 53, but they are as limited as Angel himself when it comes to imagining the human complexity of a country maid. The Clare family demonstrates the limitations of the English middle class when it comes to morality. It is their class that condemns Tess, of course, and we are much less surprised by Angel's reaction to Tess's confession because we have learned something about his origins.

There are a number of minor characters, some who appear several times in the novel and add to its highly structured plot. For instance, the reappearance of the man who paints slogans, whom Tess first meets in Chapter 12, reduces the **melodrama** of his introduction and also acts to remind us of the moral boundaries which Tess has crossed. These characters range from those who are simply incidental, to those who provide comparative and background material. Hardy uses the rougher characters to hint at a certain vulgarity or essential paganism in country life, while the idealised dairyfolk help construct a rural idyll at Talbothays.

THEMES

LOSS AND THE INEVITABILITY OF SUFFERING

As Hardy explores the human condition, so wandering, loss and the inevitability of suffering and of death become the dominant themes of the novel. Even the simple passage of time is shown, within this context, to be malign. In *Tess*, all the characters, but especially Tess herself, seem to be under the control of an external force that conspires against them – 'the President of the Immortals' (Chapter 59, p. 489).

Tess Durbeyfield is an ordinary country girl, but her life and death are affected by the fortunes of her predecessors, the ancient d'Urbervilles. She is bound to repeat and duplicate what has gone before. Tess is snared by the past, and doomed from the outset. Her death on the gallows seems both inevitable and, given that Angel is able to replace her with 'Liza-Lu, insignificant. Even as she enters the Valley of the Great Dairies, where she will be at her happiest, her position there is likened to that of 'a fly on a billiard-table of indefinite length, and of no more consequence to the surroundings than that fly' (Chapter 16, p. 159). The past, therefore, determines the present, as seen in the landscape, in communities and in individuals' lives.

Tess tries to capture and live just for the present. '"Don't think of what's past!" said she. "I am not going to think outside of now. Why should we! Who knows what tomorrow has in store?"'

CHECK THE BOOK

For a detailed discussion of the extent to which Hardy's representation of rural life was accurate, or rather whether or not it was complete, see K.D.M. Snell's *Annals of the Labouring Poor* (Cambridge University Press, 1987).

(Chapter 58, p. 480). In other words, Tess learns to reject history (Chapter 19) and the future (Chapters 15 and 19). She wants to teach this to Angel, and it is Tess who creates the space, the short period of happiness they have together. She does this, however, by a deliberate act that both makes this period possible and will inevitably bring it to an end, that is, Alec's murder. We are therefore forced to return to the supposition that the individual is never totally free to act, that their life is predestined, that passivity is preferable to wilfulness.

THE NATURAL AND CONVENTIONAL

The relationship of humanity to nature forms the second major theme of the novel. This is a complex theme within which nature and convention are juxtaposed. It is social convention which condemns Tess. What happens within The Chase would have been seen simply as a lesson learned within nature, which would have allowed her to 'veil bygones' as the 'recuperative power which pervaded organic nature was surely not denied to maidenhood alone' (Chapter 15, p. 150). People are moved to take pleasure in the world around them because of nature: 'some spirit within her rose automatically as the sap in the twigs. It was unexpended youth, surging up anew after its temporary check, and bringing with it hope, and the invincible instinct towards self-delight' (Chapter 15, p. 151). Nonetheless, nature is cruel: 'the serpent hisses where the sweet birds sing' (Chapter 12, p. 123).

CHECK THE BOOK

John Alcorn's *The Nature Novel from Hardy to Lawrence* (Macmillan, 1977) still provides a valuable guide to Hardy's use of nature in *Tess*.

Despite Hardy's apparent attack on Victorian morality, then, we can still see a certain malignity in nature as an amoral cycle. Nature is used in the novel as a presence and as an idea. In the form of seasons it helps add structure to the novel – and to people's lives. It is used as the norm against which characters and situations are judged, and as a pressure or force that acts on the characters: 'A particularly fine spring came round, and the stir of germination was almost audible in the buds; it moved her, as it moved the wild animals, and made her passionate to go' (Chapter 15, p. 150). Humanity is subject to nature.

NARRATIVE TECHNIQUES

STRUCTURE

The novel is very carefully structured around seven phases. The handling of time relies partly on season, but varies in each phase. We can see a variety of temporal scales at work in the novel, including the distant past, the recent past, insect, animal and human time. Apart from this, Hardy often uses very subtle shifts back and forward in time. For instance, when we catch up with Joan and John at Rolliver's in Chapter 4 the narrative moves back in time before moving on to the point where Tess decides to go and get them at the end of Chapter 3. On other occasions the narrative speeds on over several years, as at the end of Phase the Second. As we have already seen, it would be all too easy for the novel to fall into two halves because of the way in which Angel and Alec tussle over Tess. This helps explain Hardy's extensive use of reminders, links and cross-references within each phase, but they also add to the overall sense of pattern in Tess's life.

Tess's journeys provide an alternative structure to the seven phases of the novel. She leaves home four times and returns three times. Each time Tess leaves home – when she travels to Trantridge, Talbothays, Flintcomb-Ash, and Sandbourne – she is slightly altered, and this makes each new journey slightly different to the last. She also goes to Emminster, and finally flees to Stonehenge, from which there is no return. Important events, like her acceptance of Clare's proposal, always take place on the move. These journeys permit Hardy to weave both ancient histories and recent agricultural changes into the text, and enable him to remind us of the key incidents in Tess's life.

NARRATIVE

The settings in a novel ordinarily provide background, atmosphere, interest, they add a degree of authenticity, and in Hardy's novels can be extremely detailed. In other words they provide the novel with a degree of **verisimilitude** and **realism**. Hardy specialises in a very careful handling of scenery and season, so that time and place reinforce mood. Every detail of the hour, season or landscape echoes a shift in sensibility. Most of Hardy's settings in *Tess*

> **CHECK THE BOOK**
>
> Michael McKeon's *Theory of the Novel: A Historical Approach* (Johns Hopkins University Press, 2000) is an excellent introduction to the history of the novel.

underline Tess's development and current condition or well-being. For example, you can contrast her arrival in the Valley of the Great Dairies in Chapter 16 with her journey to Flintcomb-Ash in Chapter 42. It is therefore vital that the settings in *Tess* are appreciated in order that the themes of the novel can be understood.

When Hardy assumes that places are unknown to his readers, he goes on to describe them as if writing a travel guide. He often initially sketches a landscape from a height and at a distance and then closes in. One of the best examples of this approach is to be found at the beginning of Chapter 14. Here, Hardy provides a long description of the August harvest at Marlott and, after initially making her an anonymous figure in the landscape, gradually moves, or even zooms, in to focus on Tess as she works among the binders. This particular example actually sets up a conflict for us. Tess is the absolute focus of attention here; we cannot keep our eyes off her because she is exceptional. Yet she is supposed to be an ordinary field-woman and 'part and parcel of outdoor nature, and … not merely an object set down therein' (Chapter 14, p. 137).

POINTS OF VIEW

It is often difficult to decide through whose eyes a particular scene is being presented, and the reader must consider this very carefully because *Tess* is not presented from a single **point of view**. Hardy predominantly uses an **omniscient narrator** in *Tess*, who gives us extra information that the characters do not have access to and who adds little speculative asides, such as that at the end of Chapter 37. The author should not normally be assumed to be the narrator, but sometimes Hardy does seem to intervene. For example, the commentary on the representation of rural people in Chapter 18 overlaps with Hardy's essay on 'The Dorsetshire Labourer' in *Longman's Magazine* (1883). Hardy also often implies that he is telling a familiar local tale, creating the illusion that the story exists quite independently of its author – for example Chapter 2. Similarly, he implies that his readers will already know some of the places where the story takes place, such as the house where Tess and Angel stay in Chapter 34. In Chapter 14 he even implies that Tess is a real person. By reminding or suggesting to his readers that he is drawing on real places and stories, Hardy creates a sense of **verisimilitude**.

CHECK THE BOOK
See Herbert F. Tucker, ed., *A Companion to Victorian Literature and Culture* (Blackwell, 1999), for a good working introduction to the period.

Hardy's detailed descriptions are often seen through the eyes of the main characters, though presented in the third person. For instance, in Chapter 27 Tess is portrayed as she is seen by Angel, which sets the scene for his first proposal. In Chapter 58 Angel's and Tess's descriptions of Stonehenge add to the strangeness of the landscape. This technique is used to create a sense of involvement, especially with Tess. We know how Tess feels about her Marlott home because we see the cottage through her eyes in Chapter 3, and this helps us to understand something of her relationship with her family and her essential homelessness. Her return home in Chapter 50 similarly provides us with a particularly clear sense of how she sees the world around her; it is indicative of the emotional strain which she is under and allows us to know a little of what she feels about her history to date.

A similar technique is used to opposite effect where the narrative itself is relayed indirectly by secondary or minor characters, as in Chapter 56 when Mrs Brooks finds Alec's body, and Chapter 58 in which Tess and Angel are found asleep by the caretaker. This creates a sense of detachment from the feelings of the major characters, while at the same time involving the reader in the events themselves, which are presented to us as if they were being reported in a newspaper or during a trial. The minor characters are not directly involved with what they see and therefore help create a dispassionate yet precise picture of what has happened.

CROSS-REFERENCES, OMENS, FORESHADOWING

As has already been noted, the book has a structure built of coincidences, repetitions, omens and foreshadowings, each reliant on the others for support. Overall, we are encouraged to read Tess as doomed. But these links between past and present also provide the reader with a sense of unity, create quite subtle ironies, and help build a narrative that entraps the reader. There are many repeated incidents which take place under altered circumstances. We see Tess at work in the harvest field, the dairy, the rick yard and the open fields. The differences in her experience are highlighted by season, location and employment. Tess is dressed by her mother, then by Marian and Izz, and on both occasions she runs into Alec. Similarly, Tess is dressed up in jewels by Angel, then in finery by Alec. With

CHECK THE BOOK

For an analysis of the ways in which repetition helps to create meaning in *Tess* read J. Hillis Miller's chapter '*Tess of the D'Urbervilles*: Repetition as Immanent Design' in his *Fiction and Repetition: Seven English Novels* (Basil Blackwell, 1982).

**CHECK
THE FILM**

Roman Polanski
became fascinated
by the way in which
the novel seems to
focus on the
influence of fate in
ordinary people's
lives, and the way in
which Tess herself
always seems to
be trapped by
circumstances,
despite her beauty
and wit.

Hardy's quite pessimistic tone, these and similar coincidences help generate a pervasive atmosphere of fatalism.

Omens include quite obvious examples such as the d'Urberville coach, the crowing of the cock on their wedding day, but also the killing of the Durbeyfields' horse and the way Tess is marked from the outset by a red ribbon. Episodes and characters are carefully woven into a complex pattern and as part of this many events are explicitly prefigured. Alec's murder, for example, is foreshadowed on several occasions, especially when Tess sees herself as a murderess at the end of Chapter 4, and when she strikes him with her gauntlet in Chapter 47. But there are also more subtle or complex images that work more cumulatively. For instance, there is a thread that runs through the text which links Tess's story to the story of Adam and Eve, and makes the outcome of the novel almost inevitable. Also, on several occasions, ancient sites and ancient histories, mingled with folklore and legend, are made to equate with an inescapable fate. The numerous tracks Tess travels, the boundaries and borders she crosses, suggest not only her own slow movement along life's path, but also the gradual accumulation of generations of human experience and custom. Those customs stand in stark contrast to the alien and arbitrary railways on which the rural economy depends.

LANGUAGE AND STYLE

When you come to study the style and language of *Tess* you will find that the vocabulary, sentence structure, diction, even the tone, all vary considerably, and this is quite deliberate on Hardy's part. Characters are in part constructed through the way they speak, and when we see something from their **point of view** we catch an echo of their language in the narrative. There are also several letters and thus there is further variation of style. There is a clear shift between the spoken and the written word when Tess writes to Clare, because to write at all she has to rely on her Sixth Standard education.

Hardy's style has often been characterised as 'bad', merely picturesque and occasionally patronising. His diction can be over-Latinate and there are moments of extreme artifice in his work. Hardy was certainly worried about his writing – he sought to improve it by reading Defoe, Fielding, Addison, Scott and *The Times*. But many passages that seem to be excessively complex create a sense of immediacy, a feeling of almost being drawn into the scene so that the reader sees it as the narrator does. Hardy therefore uses very strange, long words and complex or convoluted sentences with lots of subclauses to create a heightened and more intense vision than could otherwise be achieved. Often this is meant to make us see something ordinary in a new light – **defamiliarisation**

Hardy experimented with language. He was both an observer of and a participant in the changes, issues and people he was writing about, and neither the language of the educated nor the dialect of the common people could take account of the experience of modernity that he was hoping to capture. What Hardy was searching for was a new language, a new style, which could carry both precision of observation and intensity of involvement. Hardy was therefore particularly careful in his choice of words. He was a poet as well as a novelist, and you should bear in mind that he kept revising the text, sometimes merely adding or changing a word, right up to 1912.

Hardy was able to use quite archaic language, like 'Verily' (Chapter 12, p. 123), classical references and foreign words, and chose to attempt a very 'literary' style, because he could expect a highly educated audience for his work. It is also interesting to see how he used this kind of language in such a way as to reflect Angel's character and breeding. Hardy is able to hint at Angel's increasing influence over Tess when her own speech begins to shift towards a more elevated style that is reminiscent of the highly educated tones of the Clare family. This is noticed by Alec, who similarly adopts some of Angel's more religious turns of phrase (in Phase the Sixth – The Convert), in sharp and often direct contrast to his more usual urban slang. As Angel builds on Tess's schooling, while her family and the other working women continue to use the dialect, she continues to speak the dialect at home, and we get a very clear picture of the way in which Tess lives in two worlds.

CHECK THE BOOK

For more on Hardy's language and style, refer to Ralph W. V. Elliott's detailed study *Thomas Hardy's English* (Basil Blackwell, 1986).

At his best, Hardy can create quite sinister effects through the odd juxtaposition of familiar words. His use of the present tense provides a very direct experience of the landscapes he described. You should look out for carefully worked and **ironical** similes in *Tess*, and what might be called Hardy's film-like technique.

Sometimes when he writes very simply he uses rhythm to stress the monotony in his characters' lives, or to give a feeling of having no choice, of fatalism. His writing is often heavily punctuated 'as if to give pause while that word was driven well home to the reader's heart' (Chapter 12, p. 128). He generally gives a quite **naturalistic** rendering to speech, but at times he creates a feeling of intensity through the sense that what they say is measured as if by a beat, especially in dialect, and when people are dealing with very stressful situations he tends to use quite **melodramatic** diction. In other words, the question of prose is not really about having a 'good' style, but about whether or not that style works for the author.

**CHECK
THE BOOK**

In *The Nature Novel
from Hardy to
Lawrence*
(Macmillan, 1977)
John Alcorn argues
that Tess's story is
encapsulated by her
movement across
the land.

IMAGERY AND SYMBOLISM

Many or even most of the symbols that we come across in the novel are really omens, but Hardy's narrative often gives the impression of something seen rather than felt. Hardy is an acute observer. Because of his sensitivity to the visual, Hardy often uses very graphic effects, such as slogans writ large in red paint, for instance, through which he sets up clear moral boundaries, but he equally draws on the subtlest of signs, such as little marks of wear and tear on buildings or furniture which indicate the passage of time at the human level.

It is worth noting Hardy's use of classical mythology to get round touchier subjects. Within the context of rural life, Hardy juxtaposes villagers with demigods. This is particularly apparent in his description of the dance at Chaseborough in Chapter 10. Dance for Hardy reveals a community's ability to survive and the degree of its coherence. The fact that this particular dance takes place eerily in an out-of-the-way barn, in which the dancers are likened to 'a sort of vegeto-human pollen' (Chapter 10, p. 107), is in itself indicative of

Trantridge's degraded condition. But the scene is also suggestive of the passions of pagan nature. Like Alec's cigar smoke, or the fog in The Chase, the haze of hay dust is simultaneously ephemeral and bewildering.

Tess is always closely associated with one of the most pervasive images in the text: the colour red. Tess, in a sense, becomes bloodstained. At the opening of the novel she stands out among the other girls because she is wearing a red ribbon against the white background of her dress. When Angel Clare first sees her he sees that red ribbon. Soon after this she is bathed in Prince's blood and thereafter becomes surrounded by red; even the d'Urberville home is built of red brick. The red that surrounds her is also contained within her, though, as we see when our attention is drawn to the redness of her snake-like mouth. Alec describes her lips as the bright red of holly berries. When she finally kills Alec our attention is drawn to the red on white of his blood on the lodging-house ceiling, which grows until it 'had the appearance of a gigantic ace of hearts' (Chapter 56, p. 471). Images and omens do not simply accumulate in this novel, however, they also converge.

CHECK THE FILM
Prince's death is omitted from Roman Polanski's 1979 film, though it is crucial in Hardy's representation of Tess's journey.

At first, when she dances at the club-walking, Tess is not only mostly white she is also sun-blessed, and this imagery works alongside her redness until sun and blood come together in Phase the Seventh – Fulfilment. The sun shines sweetly on Tess while she is still a girl, and continues to do so while she works at the dairy. The summer suns bring fertility and bounty to Talbothays, which is where Tess ripens into fully formed womanhood and where she is happiest. But the sun does not always shine. Tess and Angel court during the misty, cold, watery hours before dawn, and at these times Tess is spiritually elevated for Clare: she is the celibate Artemis, 'a visionary essence of woman' (Chapter 20, p. 187), only becoming the physical dairymaid that she really is when the sun rises. When Tess finally agrees to marry Angel their lives are held in the balance at the equinox. They finally wed in the middle of winter, close to the longest night. The sun deserts and finally betrays Tess. It becomes a force that stains or marks her, like her red ribbon and the blood of the horse. 'The sun was so low on that short last afternoon of the year that it shone in through a small opening and formed a golden staff which stretched across to her skirt, where it made a spot like a paint-mark set upon her' (Chapter 34, p. 284). The final curtain falls on her as she sleeps in a bed hung about by crimson drapes, revealed by a 'shaft of dazzling sunlight' (Chapter 57, p. 478).

PART FOUR

CRITICAL HISTORY

RECEPTION AND EARLY CRITICAL REVIEWS

Tess of the d'Urbervilles: A Pure Woman was not well received by critics when it was first published. The *Quarterly Review* declared that the subtitle put 'a strain upon the English language'. *The Independent* said that the novel was 'a pretty kettle of fish for pure people to eat' and that it threatened 'the moral fibre of young readers'. *Punch, or the London Charivari* produced a satire of the novel in 1892. Called 'Bo and the Blacksheep', this was a one-page pastiche of the novel in which Bonduca, or Bo Peep, 'had a flexuous and finely-drawn figure not unreminiscent of many a vanished night and dame.'

Thus, the contemporary critics largely focused on the question of Hardy's morality. A few preferred to concentrate on the issue of Hardy's style or the plausibility of the story, but most critics attacked Hardy as a libertine because of the novel's subject matter and because he had chosen to describe Tess as 'pure' in the subtitle. An unmarried woman, who had lost her virginity, had an illegitimate child and become entangled in an ultimately adulterous relationship leading to murder could not be 'pure' in the view of most readers.

Hardy thought that the critics were reading his novel too literally and argued:

> I still maintain that her innate purity remained intact to the very last; though I frankly own that a certain outward purity left her on her last fall. I regarded her then as being in the hands of circumstances, not morally responsible, a mere corpse drifting with the current.

LATER CRITICISM

Despite the highly controversial start to the novel's career, *Tess* rapidly became, and still is, very popular. What becomes

CONTEXT

Punch's satire 'Mr. Punch's Agricultural Novel. Bo and the Blacksheep. A story of *the Sex'* by 'Thomas of Wessex' was published on 7 May 1892. It concludes: 'And, from the calm nonchalance of a Wessex hamlet, another novel was launched into a world of reviews, where the multitude of readers is not as to their external displacements, but as to their subjective experiences.'

CHECK THE FILM

Roman Polanski focuses on Tess as 'a pure woman', her naturalness and her response to nature. Polanski therefore picks up on Hardy's apparent criticism of Victorian society, but he then shifts emphasis, in comparison to the novel, by extending that criticism by implication to encompass any and all repressive environs.

CHECK THE BOOK

To put *Tess* into the wider context of Victorian literature and its history of criticism, see Francis O'Gorman, ed., *The Victorian Novel* (Blackwell, 2002).

particularly clear when we look at the various and often contesting readings of *Tess*, though, is that both Tess and *Tess* are equally heterogeneous. Today it is Angel who is more likely to be attacked than Tess herself. Many critics have in fact found it hard to believe in the double standard to which Tess falls victim. They suggest that Hardy might be able to convince us that Angel is a prig or a hypocrite, but wonder that Angel cannot see any resemblance at all between his past and Tess's. As critics have come to focus on the theme of 'the deadly war between flesh and spirit', as Hardy described it in his Preface to *Jude the Obscure* (1895), so they have succumbed to what has been described as 'obsessive Angel-baiting'.

Hardy languished for many years in partial obscurity as a fairly minor writer. Seen as a self-taught peasant, he was predominantly thought of as a quaint local author who catalogued the decay of a vanishing, more rural way of life, who was good at dialect and faintly hostile to new industrial technologies. Critics therefore focused on his detailed accounts of folklore and village or local custom. He was seen as a good regional novelist who wrote about and came from the peasantry. Wessex is still widely sold to tourists via Hardy's writing.

If we accept this approach, *Tess* might be seen as the culmination of Hardy's best work about the countryside. Tess's tragedy lies in her anomalous social position, caused by her d'Urberville blood, a position which represents the tragedy of rural England in which the old aristocracy gives way to a new urban elite, who do not understand or care for the land and its people.

Similarly, *Tess* has frequently been read as being about the fall of the English peasantry, in which case Tess becomes the representative of that peasantry, sent away from the idyllic world of her childhood to become the victim of Alec, son of a successful merchant. Once out of his clutches, she is then subject to Angel, the urban intellectual, and slave to the needs of the threshing machine, which is symbolic of her final and complete degradation as caused by the invasion of everything that is out of sympathy with the rhythms of rural life.

A new approach finally emerged when the cultural materialists reappraised Hardy in the 1970s. They saw him as a major author, whose chief merit lay in his sympathetic treatment and understanding of the labourer, and as an author who could represent the key issues of the modern age.

Though Hardy was not of the labouring class himself, they saw him as a radical author, critical of class relations, as characterised by Tess's subjection to economic need and abuse. These critics also highlighted the importance of historical context by pointing out that the English peasantry were long gone by the time that Hardy was writing. By the 1870s, they argue, the countryside was already structured by social mobility, hence Tess's use of dialect with her family – self-employed hagglers – and standard English with her 'betters'. And, they stress, Hardy was well aware of the appalling conditions of rural life in the 1870s; it is clear, for instance, that the Durbeyfields exist only on the barest margins of economic survival.

Many critics have persisted in focusing on Hardy's concept of community despite this, and the text is still widely and simply praised for its accuracy and **verisimilitude** in respect of rural life. But some well-considered arguments have emerged against this reading, which stress that it is not meant to be a representative or **realist** text. The cultural materialist reading of *Tess* as social criticism has not convinced all subsequent critics, but – and this is related to their new approach – many have come to focus to a greater extent on Hardy's philosophy and ideology.

CHECK
THE BOOK
G. Harvey and
N. Tredell, eds.,
trace the history of
Tess criticism from
its origins to the
present day in
*Thomas Hardy: Tess
of the d'Urbervilles*
(Palgrave
Macmillan, 2002).

CONTEMPORARY APPROACHES

A key reading that has recently gained currency among a number of critics is one which focuses on Tess as the last of an ancient line, not as the last of an ancient and venerable aristocracy, but as the daughter of a decayed and degenerate race. The influence of Darwin's evolutionary theory on Hardy's thought is drawn out in the way in which Tess seems to repeat or is subject to the acts of her ancestors. She is haunted, not only by the d'Urberville coach, but also by the portraits of the d'Urberville women which Angel cannot get out of his mind after Tess's confession, and whom she physically and mentally resembles. She takes on the appearance of a lady when

CHECK
THE BOOK
For an excellent
example of feminist
criticism, see Judith
Weissman, *Half
Savage and Hardy
and Free: Women
and Rural
Radicalism in the
Nineteenth-Century
Novel* (Wesleyan
University Press,
1987).

she is dressed in the jewels Angel gives her, her figure is finer than any of the other working women and she, like her father, is often quite conceited. This Darwinian subtext is said to provide an alternative, **naturalist** voice in the novel which undercuts much of Hardy's defence of Tess as a simple peasant maid who is a victim of her society. She often acts wilfully because of a misplaced sense of pride, and when she remains passive her fate seems to be determined as much by her heredity as her environment.

Related to this, Hardy is often seen as a pessimist. But this assessment largely depends upon the critic's understanding of Hardy's conception of the human spirit, of fate, his themes of wandering and isolation, the war between flesh and spirit. It is because of these themes that he has been classified by some as an early modernist. Tess is sensitive to the modern condition and this supports their case, as does the fact that she is not solely a victim, but a much more complex character who cannot be pinned down. She is a victim and a murderess. Of course, many critics have continued to treat Tess as if she were a real person despite this, in part because Hardy encourages this process. For instance, they still ask, 'Was she seduced or was she raped?'

Hardy clearly worked hard at defending Tess's purity and the morality of the novel itself, and many critics have now come to realise that in putting Tess, in a sense, on trial, it is 'purity' itself and the right to define it that is in fact tried. If the novel is read in this way, it is actually possible to see *Tess of the d'Urbervilles* as a feminist text. This is because the society that damns Tess as impure is essentially patriarchal. She is too complex a woman to be understood by a society that classifies women under the headings 'virgin' or 'whore'. Hardy is very much in love with his 'Tessy' and as such cannot condone what happens to her. We may of course then wonder whether he succeeds in handling the issues he raises, but that is a separate question.

Many feminist critics still consider the novel to be entirely misogynistic. They argue that Tess is treated as spectacle in the novel and is presented to us as an object for display. Tess is looked at in detail, from near and far; we gaze into the depths of her eyes,

CONTEXT

Modernism developed in the arts from the end of the nineteenth century and included a variety of movements; it involved a reaction against representational art, the rejection of traditional forms and subjects, so that modernists were often experimental with both form and content.

we see her working as a figure in the landscape, we consider her every 'aspect'. This is partly because she is a woman, they suggest, and women are exhibited as objects for the male gaze within patriarchy, but Hardy's heightened visual approach underlines this process and makes it especially forceful.

Hardy's architectural training has been seen as influencing the structure of his novels, but we can also see that it has reinforced his visual acuity. Tess is situated within a landscape that is visually opened up and made accessible to the reader by Hardy, and described as if he were a travel writer or explorer of far-flung, exotic lands. This is why *Tess* is still so closely associated with Hardy's rich descriptive narrative and detailed observation of rural life.

CONTEXT

Taken from feminist psychoanalytic film theory, 'the male gaze' suggests that women are **objectified** within patriarchy. It links the **subjectivity** and subjection of women to the process of representation and the pleasure of looking. Femininity is formed through spectacle, masculinity through the gaze.

PART FIVE

BACKGROUND

THOMAS HARDY

Thomas Hardy (1840–1928) is often mistakenly described as a self-taught peasant. He was, however, the son of a builder and master mason who employed at least six men, had an excellent formal education and had already become a successful architect before he entered the literary circles of his day. Hardy therefore certainly moved up the social ladder during his life, but he never entirely belonged to the labouring class to which his family was only ever tangentially connected. When he wrote, he wrote about labourers as a somewhat distanced observer; he did not write for them but for the educated metropolitan public.

CHECK THE NET
The Victorian Web –
**http://www.
victorianweb.org/**
– has extensive
commentaries and
further background
information on *Tess
of the d'Urbervilles,*
Thomas Hardy and
his period.

Hardy was born in the hamlet Higher Bockhampton near Dorchester. Initially he attended a village school and was encouraged to read Dryden's *Aeneid* and Johnson's *Rasselas* by his mother. He went on to attend Dorchester High School until he was sixteen. Then from 1856 to 1862 he was apprenticed to John Hicks, a local architect, and became the friend of poet and antiquarian William Barnes. Once he had completed his apprenticeship, he went on to work at the architectural offices of Arthur Blomfield in London.

By this point, between 1862 and 1867, Hardy had become a prize-winning architect and was trying to get his poetry published, but he was also beginning to lose his Christian faith under the influence of Charles Darwin's *Origin of Species* and *Essays and Reviews*. As he was also suffering from poor health he went back to work for John Hicks in Dorchester. His health recovered and he began writing his first, unpublished, novel, *The Poor Man and the Lady*. When Hicks died in 1869 Hardy was offered a position at the firm's Weymouth office, which is where he began to write his first published novel, *Desperate Remedies* (1871). During 1871 Hardy also met his first wife, Emma Lavinia Gifford, whom he was able to marry after the successful publication of *Far from the Madding Crowd*, in 1874.

Thomas and Emma Hardy initially lived in the West Country, then moved to London for three years in 1878. In 1881 they returned to Dorset and in 1885 settled at Max Gate on the edge of Dorchester, where they lived for the rest of their lives. However, they always kept up the habit of returning to London for the three months after Easter that constituted 'the season'. The marriage was not happy, a fact that is supposedly reflected in *Jude the Obscure* (1895), but they kept busy and travelled widely.

After the mixed critical reception of *Jude*, Hardy gave up novel writing entirely in favour of poetry. He published prolifically during the last thirty years of his life and by the time that Emma Hardy died in 1912, Thomas Hardy had become a celebrated English author. Hardy continued living at Max Gate and, in 1914, married Florence Emily Dugdale (1879–1937). With her help, he destroyed many of his letters and journals and prepared two, quite misleading, volumes on his life, *The Early Life of Thomas Hardy, 1840–1891* (1928) and *The Later Years of Thomas Hardy, 1892–1928* (1930). Both were published after his death under his wife's name.

CHECK THE BOOK
Useful contextual material on other Victorians' perceptions of Hardy and the reception of his work can be found in James Gibson, ed., *Thomas Hardy: Interviews and Recollections* (Macmillan, 1999).

OTHER WORKS

Tess of the d'Urbervilles (1891) was preceded by *Desperate Remedies* (1871), *Under the Greenwood Tree* (1872), *A Pair of Blue Eyes* (1873), *Far from the Madding Crowd* (1874), *The Hand of Ethelberta* (1876), *The Return of the Native* (1878), *The Trumpet-Major* (1880), *A Laodicean* (1881), *Two on a Tower* (1882), *The Mayor of Casterbridge* (1886) and *The Woodlanders* (1887). *Tess* was followed by *The Well-Beloved* (1897), written several years earlier, and by Hardy's last novel, *Jude the Obscure* (1895). Hardy also published many short stories, including several collections: *Wessex Tales* (1888), *A Group of Noble Dames* (1891), *Life's Little Ironies* (1894), and *A Changed Man and Other Tales* (1913).

When writing *Tess*, Hardy often drew on his earlier work, which supplied him with incidental characters and local detail. For instance, William Dewy is a character in *Under the Greenwood Tree*, while the conjurors Fall and Trendle appear in *The Mayor of Casterbridge* and 'The Withered Arm' in *Wessex Tales* respectively. Hardy was a prose-writer too and his best-known essay 'The

Dorsetshire Labourer' published in *Longman's Magazine* in July 1883 was used extensively in *Tess* to provide social commentary and particularly in the discussion of 'Hodge'. There are echoes of *Tess* in Hardy's poetry, including 'Proud Songsters' (1928) and a poem about Tess herself: 'Tess's Lament'.

HISTORICAL BACKGROUND

CHECK THE NET

Carry out your own documentary research by going to The Archives Hub at **http://www. archiveshub.ac.uk/**

Hardy centres *Tess* in and around Dorset, an agricultural region which, by the time that Hardy was writing, had already undergone considerable economic and social change. There was no longer a 'peasantry', but a society structured by class relations and social mobility. The rural economy was dependent upon urban markets – Dorset, which was a pastoral county, did especially well out of this – and by the 1890s had just been through a long-term depression brought about by shifts in the global economy. As a result of this depression, employment had declined drastically and wages had fallen, especially in the south and east of England where arable farming predominated. Gross output fell even in Dorset, despite its specialisation in dairy production, and some tenant farmers in Dorset refused to bind themselves to anything longer than a one-year lease. Thousands had left the countryside in search of work, and a series of education acts passed from the 1870s onwards added to the process of depopulation. There were eighteen thousand agricultural labourers in Dorset in 1871 and only twelve and a half thousand by 1891. The Dorset agricultural labourer lived, generally, in appalling conditions, some of the worst, in fact, in the country, while class relations were among the most embittered of the time.

CHECK THE BOOK

For more on the history of rural England at the time that Hardy was writing, see Alun Howkins, *Reshaping Rural England: A Social History 1850–1925* (HarperCollins, 1991).

Late nineteenth-century rural society was structured by mobility, insecurity, separation, just like its urban counterpart. We can see this in Tess's constant journeying and movement from farm to farm, but also in the journeys of more minor characters like Marian and Izz, or the way in which the Durbeyfields are thrown out of their home as soon as the last tenant dies, because they are morally inferior. The agricultural revolution had been and gone by the time that Hardy was writing – the railway came to Dorchester when Hardy was seven. What he describes, therefore, is an ongoing, continuous process of change in the countryside, not a static and idealised rural world, a **pastoral** destroyed by new, invasive technologies. Hardy was sensitive to the workings of the rural economy and to its actual, everyday social relations – though not the most violent of these. Crucially, what Hardy therefore represents in terms of history or social background is not, as such, the reality of things like field labour. He was not always accurate in terms of detail (a woman would not have worked on a threshing machine in the late 1880s as Tess does); what concerned him was the economic context of that work and the impact of the wider social and moral concerns of his period on people like the Durbeyfields.

LITERARY **BACKGROUND**

Hardy's literary antecedents include the Romantics, **realists** like George Eliot and the 'rural' authors of his day. What is interesting about Hardy, however, is that he seems to move beyond many of his forebears. For instance, Hardy is critical of the Romantics' view of nature – 'Some people would like to know whence the poet whose philosophy is in these days deemed as profound … gets his authority for speaking of "Nature's holy plan".' And while, in a way, he returns to their vision of nature, which was actually quite hellish, he also sets out to place it within a modern context and undermine both their conception of Providence, and of self-determination.

Books about the countryside proliferated at the end of the century. The desire to read about rural life came about as the countryside became more remote from metropolitan audiences and threatened by competition from abroad, then depression and depopulation. Authors like Richard Jefferies (1848–87) – *Hodge and His Masters* (1880) and *The Toilers of the Field* (1881), and *The Dewy Morn* (1884) – provided a catalogue of apparently genuine peasants for their readers to enjoy in prose, fiction and verse, while the Baedeker guides of the time documented the details of rural life for the growing tourist industry.

Hardy can be just as silent as any other country author about the horrors of rural life, and frequently slips into the stereotypical

> **CONTEXT**
>
> The term Romanticism covers a range of tendencies in literature, art and culture that emerged at the end of the eighteenth century and dominated the early years of the nineteenth century. It generally involved a movement away from the sceptical, rational, formal culture of the eighteenth century and aimed to liberate the creative imagination.

CONTEXT

The Baedeker guides were established by Karl Baedeker (1801–59) in 1839. Popular on the continent, the English-language version soon dominated the British market for tour books.

CHECK THE BOOK

Jeff Nunokawa argues that the influence of Baedeker guides on Hardy's writing can be directly documented. See Nunokawa's 'Tess, tourism, and the spectacle of the woman' in Linda M. Shires, ed., *Rewriting the Victorians: Theory, History and the Politics of Gender* (Routledge, 1992).

portrayal of 'Hodge' that he criticised in 'The Dorsetshire Labourer'. He describes panoramic views of Wessex that would have done Baedeker proud and captures them for the armchair tourist who wants to preserve a vanishing, primitive way of life. Tess, however, is not a flat caricature of a seduced peasant girl, but a complex figure who cannot be categorised. She is certainly put on display, at times she does seem to be a tourist attraction who just catches the roving eye, but Tess is also viewed from all possible angles.

Genre

Given the stress on fate, coupled with the biological and sociological pressures that are placed on the characters, the novel might be categorised as naturalist. **Naturalism** expresses a post-Darwinian view of life in which human beings are seen as fundamentally no more than specialised animals, subject to natural forces such as heredity and environment. Naturalists see the novel as a kind of experiment and claim a degree of scientific accuracy for their work. Typical subject matter is the miserable and poverty-stricken, or those driven by animal appetites such as hunger or sexuality. Life is seen as a squalid and meaningless tragedy. However, this is unworkable given the poetic *tableaux*, mythical and **metaphysical** elements that are also found within *Tess*.

Neither is *Tess* a **realist** novel. Realists aimed to present 'things as they are' and in the nineteenth century most realist novels consisted of a detailed representation of life and depiction of human nature as it really is. 'Realism', Hardy said, 'is not art'. Though the novel is easily paraphrased, is sometimes **expository**, and though most of its **foreshadowed** discoveries and turning points are tied up by the end, it does not have the happy ending of a classic realist text; instead 'Liza-Lu steps in to take Tess's place by Clare's side as Tess herself is hanged. *Tess* is about isolation and separation, the condition of modernity. Hardy's 'realism' is therefore simply a literary device which helps him to outline Tess's joy, stoicism, or humiliation.

World events	Thomas Hardy's life	Literary events
		1798–1844 Heyday of British Romantic movement
		1832 Death of Sir Walter Scott
1834 Union workhouses established. Transportation to Australia of Tolpuddle martyrs		**1834** William Harrison Ainsworth, *Rookwood*
1837 Accession of Queen Victoria		
1838 Formation of Anti-Corn Law League		
	1839 Thomas Hardy, mason, marries Jemima Hand, cook	
	1840 Birth of **Thomas Hardy**, their eldest son, at Higher Bockhampton, Dorset	**1840** Birth of Emile Zola
		1844 William Barnes, *Poems of Rural Life in the Dorset Dialect*
1846 Repeal of Corn Laws		
1847 Railway comes to Dorchester		
	1848 Attends village school	**1848** Ainsworth, *The Lancashire Witches*; birth of Richard Jefferies
		1850 Birth of Guy de Maupassant; death of William Wordsworth; Nathaniel Hawthorne, *The Scarlet Letter*
1851 The Great Exhibition shows first reaping and threshing machines		
1854–6 Crimean War		**1855** Death of Charlotte Brontë
	1856–62 Apprenticed to architect John Hicks. Witnesses public hanging of Martha Brown, Dorchester	**1857** Gustave Flaubert, *Madame Bovary*

World events	Thomas Hardy's life	Literary events
		1859 Charles Darwin, *On the Origin of Species by Means of Natural Selection*
		1860 George Eliot, *The Mill on the Floss*
		1861 Charles Dickens, *Great Expectations*; Eliot, *Silas Marner*
	1862–7 Works in London as architect. Begins to lose religious faith	
	1867 Returns to Dorchester to work for Hicks. Begins working on *The Poor Man and the Lady* (now lost)	**1866** Fyodor Dostoevsky, *Crime and Punishment*
	1869 Moves to Weymouth to work for architect Crickmay. Begins writing *Desperate Remedies*	
1870 Forster's Education Act; elementary education for all; from hereon depopulation of Dorset countryside; from this date county moves from general use of the life lease option to 1-year leases	**1870** Restoring St Juliot's church, north Cornwall, Hardy meets his future wife, Emma Lavinia Gifford	
	1871 Publishes *Desperate Remedies*	**1871–2** Eliot, *Middlemarch*
	1872 Publishes *Under the Greenwood Tree*	
	1873 Publishes *A Pair of Blue Eyes*; *Far from the Madding Crowd* serialised	
1874–80 Disraeli prime minister	**1874** *Far from the Madding Crowd* published. Marries Emma	
	1876 They go to live at Sturminster Newton. *The Hand of Ethelberta* published	
		1877 Henry James, *The American*; Leo Tolstoy, *Anna Karenina*
	1878 *The Return of the Native* published	

World events	Thomas Hardy's life	Literary events
	1880 *The Trumpet-Major* published. Very ill for six months	**1880** Richard Jefferies, *Hodge and his Masters*; Maupassant, *Boule de Suif* (*Ball of Fat*)
	1881 Publishes *A Laodicean*	**1881** Jefferies, *Toilers of the Field*
	1882 Visits Paris after publishing *Two on a Tower*	
	1883 'The Dorsetshire Labourer' published	
1884 Foundation of Fabian Society		**1884** Jefferies, *The Dewy Morn*
1885 Siege of Khartoum		
	1886 *The Mayor of Casterbridge* published	
	1887 *The Woodlanders* published	**1887** Zola, *La Terre* (*Earth*)
1888 Six Jack the Ripper murders in London's East End	**1888** *Wessex Tales* published	**1890** James Frazer, *The Golden Bough*
1891 Free education in England	**1891** *A Group of Noble Dames* published; first serialised edition of **Tess of the d'Urbervilles** published	
	1894 *Life's Little Ironies* published	
	1896 *Jude the Obscure* published	
	1897 *The Well-Beloved* published	
	1898 *Wessex Poems*, his first collection of verse, published	
1899–1902 Boer War	**1904** First part of *The Dynasts* published. Definitive edition of *Tess of the d'Urbervilles*	
	1912 Death of Emma	
1914–18 First World War	**1914** Marries Florence Emily Dugdale, his secretary	
	1928 Death of Thomas Hardy	

John Alcorn, *The Nature Novel from Hardy to Lawrence*, Macmillan, 1977

Diana Basham, *The Trial of Woman: Feminism and the Occult Sciences in Victorian Literature and Society*, Macmillan, 1992

Gillian Beer, *Darwin's Plots: Evolutionary Narrative in Darwin, George Eliot and Nineteenth-Century Fiction*, second edition, Cambridge University Press, 2000

Ralph W. V. Elliott, *Thomas Hardy's English*, Basil Blackwell, 1986

Marjorie Garson, *Hardy's Fables of Integrity: Woman, Body, Text*, Clarendon Press, 1991

Simon Gatrell, *Thomas Hardy and the Proper Study of Mankind*, Macmillan, 1993

James Gibson, ed., *Thomas Hardy: Interviews and Recollections*, Macmillan, 1999

John Goode, 'Woman and the Literary Text' in Juliet Mitchell and Ann Oakley, eds., *The Rights and Wrongs of Women*, Penguin, 1976

John Goode, *Thomas Hardy, The Offensive Truth*, Blackwell, 1988

G. Harvey and N. Tredell, eds., *Thomas Hardy: Tess of the d'Urbervilles*, Palgrave Macmillan, 2002

J. Hillis Miller, *Fiction and Repetition: Seven English Novels*, Basil Blackwell, 1982
See his chapter 'Tess of the D'Urbervilles: Repetition as Immanent Design'

Alun Howkins, *Reshaping Rural England: A Social History 1850–1925*, HarperCollins, 1991

A. M. Jackson, *Illustration and the Novels of Thomas Hardy*, Rowman and Littlefield, 1981

James R. Kincaid, *Child-Loving: The Erotic Child and Victorian Culture*, Routledge, 1992

J. T. Laird, *The Shaping of Tess of the d'Urbervilles*, Oxford University Press, 1975
For an account of the formation of the novel

Michael McKeon, ed., *Theory of the Novel: A Historical Approach*, Johns Hopkins University Press, 2000

Kevin Moore, *The Descent of the Imagination: Post-Romantic Culture in the Later Novels of Thomas Hardy*, New York University Press, 1990

Rosemarie Morgan, *Women and Sexuality in the Novels of Thomas Hardy*, Routledge, 1988

Ross C. Murfin, *Swinburne, Hardy, Lawrence and the Burden of Belief*, University of Chicago Press, 1978

Jeff Nunokawa, '*Tess*, tourism, and the spectacle of the woman' in Linda M. Shires, ed., *Rewriting the Victorians: Theory, History and the Politics of Gender*, Routledge, 1992

Francis O'Gorman, ed., *The Victorian Novel*, Blackwell, 2002

H. P. Owen, *Concepts of Deity*, Macmillan, 1971

Toni Reed, *Demon-Lovers and Their Victims in British Fiction*, University Press of Kentucky, 1988

Harriet Ritvo, *The Animal Estate: The English and Other Creatures in Victorian England*, Penguin, 1990

K. D. M. Snell, *Annals of the Labouring Poor: Social Change and Agrarian England, 1660–1900*, Cambridge University Press, 1987

Rebecca Stott, *The Fabrication of the Late-Victorian Femme Fatale: The Kiss of Death*, Macmillan, 1992
> For an account of Hardy's self-censorship

J. A. Sutherland, *Victorian Novelists and Publishers*, Athlone Press, 1976

Tony Tanner, 'Colour and Movement in Hardy's *Tess of the d'Urbervilles*' in Ian Watt, ed., *The Victorian Novel, Modern Essays in Criticism*, Oxford University Press, 1971

Herbert F. Tucker, ed., *A Companion to Victorian Literature and Culture*, Blackwell, 1999

Judith Weissman, *Half Savage and Hardy and Free: Women and Rural Radicalism in the Nineteenth-Century Novel*, Wesleyan University Press, 1987

Merryn Williams, *Thomas Hardy and Rural England*, Macmillan, 1972

Raymond Williams, *The Country and the City*, Oxford University Press, 1973

Raymond Williams, *The English Novel from Dickens to Lawrence*, Hogarth, 1984

anthropomorphic human attributes ascribed to something that is not human

closure the feeling of completeness and finality achieved by the ending of some literary works; especially associated with the classic realist texts of the nineteenth century

defamiliarisation 'making strange'; Hardy's writing can often strip away everything that is familiar about the world, so that we see it anew. This can be referred to as estrangement or defamiliarisation

denouement final unfolding of the plot

expository from 'exposition', i.e. an explanation or to do with the delivery of information

flashback narrative technique that disrupts time sequence by introducing an event or memory which happened in the past prior to the present action of the novel

foreshadow prefigure a later event or turning point. This literary technique is used extensively by Hardy

gothic a popular form that emerged in the eighteenth century, during the nineteenth century the gothic went through an architectural and stylistic revival that was often linked to medievalism. In literary form, its eerie and fantastic devices were often used in sensation fiction and other popular Victorian genres

irony covert sarcasm; saying one thing while meaning another; using words to convey the opposite of their literal meaning; saying something that has one meaning for someone knowledgeable about a situation and another meaning for those who are not; incongruity between what might be expected and what actually happens; ill-timed arrival of an event which had been hoped for

melodramatic a melodrama was originally a popular play with music which aimed to excite the audience through incident and strong but simple feelings, and with characters who were clearly 'good' or 'bad' and an ending that was always happy

metaphorical from metaphor – figure of speech in which a descriptive term, or name or action characteristic of one object is applied to another to suggest a likeness between, but which does not use 'like' or 'as' in the comparison

metaphysical to do with the immaterial, or philosophy that there is something beyond or independent of the human, the abstract, sometimes the supernatural

naturalism a form of **realism**

neologism coinage of a new word or expression

objectified made into, or looked at, as an object or image; made into a spectacle

omniscient narrator storyteller with total, God-like knowledge of the characters and their actions

pastoral literature about an idealised rural life. Written from the **point of view**, but also often critical, of the city. The implication is that rural life is simpler and more wholesome than urban life

pathos suffering feeling; that quality in a work of art that arouses pity and sadness

point of view seen from the viewpoint or through the eyes of a particular character

psychomachea a medieval morality play in which vice and virtue battle for the soul of Everyman. Derived from a poem by Prudentius, 'Psychomachia', c.400, which in the Greek means 'a struggle or fight for life'

realist a realist author represents the world as it is rather than as it should be, using description rather than invention; observes and documents everyday life in straightforward prose; draws on characters from all levels of society, but often from the lowest classes; represents their speech and manners accurately. Realism became the dominant form of literature in the nineteenth century

subjectivity the 'subject' is used in a specialised way here to refer to the individual as understood in western capitalist society. Individuals possess subjectivity, in the sense of feeling and thinking freely and independently, but they are also 'subjected', in the sense of being in abeyance to authority: they are politically 'subject', i.e. not really free at all

verisimilitude giving the appearance of truth or reality

Karen Sayer lectures in the Department of History at Trinity and All Saints College, University of Leeds. She took her first degree at Portsmouth Polytechnic and was awarded her D.Phil. at the University of Sussex. Her first monograph, *Women of the Fields,* was published by Manchester University Press in 1995; her second, *Country Cottages: A Cultural History,* was published by Manchester University Press in 2000.

General editor

Martin Gray, former Head of the Department of English Studies at the University of Stirling, and of Literary Studies at the University of Luton

Maya Angelou
I Know Why the Caged Bird Sings

Jane Austen
Pride and Prejudice

Alan Ayckbourn
Absent Friends

Elizabeth Barrett Browning
Selected Poems

Robert Bolt
A Man for All Seasons

Harold Brighouse
Hobson's Choice

Charlotte Brontë
Jane Eyre

Emily Brontë
Wuthering Heights

Shelagh Delaney
A Taste of Honey

Charles Dickens
David Copperfield
Great Expectations
Hard Times
Oliver Twist

Roddy Doyle
Paddy Clarke Ha Ha Ha

George Eliot
Silas Marner
The Mill on the Floss

Anne Frank
The Diary of a Young Girl

William Golding
Lord of the Flies

Oliver Goldsmith
She Stoops to Conquer

Willis Hall
The Long and the Short and the Tall

Thomas Hardy
Far from the Madding Crowd
The Mayor of Casterbridge
Tess of the d'Urbervilles
The Withered Arm and other Wessex Tales

L.P. Hartley
The Go-Between

Seamus Heaney
Selected Poems

Susan Hill
I'm the King of the Castle

Barry Hines
A Kestrel for a Knave

Louise Lawrence
Children of the Dust

Harper Lee
To Kill a Mockingbird

Laurie Lee
Cider with Rosie

Arthur Miller
The Crucible
A View from the Bridge

Robert O'Brien
Z for Zachariah

Frank O'Connor
My Oedipus Complex and Other Stories

George Orwell
Animal Farm

J.B. Priestley
An Inspector Calls
When We Are Married

Willy Russell
Educating Rita
Our Day Out

J.D. Salinger
The Catcher in the Rye

William Shakespeare
Henry IV Part I
Henry V
Julius Caesar
Macbeth
The Merchant of Venice
A Midsummer Night's Dream
Much Ado About Nothing

Romeo and Juliet
The Tempest
Twelfth Night

George Bernard Shaw
Pygmalion

Mary Shelley
Frankenstein

R.C. Sherriff
Journey's End

Rukshana Smith
Salt on the snow

John Steinbeck
Of Mice and Men

Robert Louis Stevenson
Dr Jekyll and Mr Hyde

Jonathan Swift
Gulliver's Travels

Robert Swindells
Daz 4 Zoe

Mildred D. Taylor
Roll of Thunder, Hear My Cry

Mark Twain
Huckleberry Finn

James Watson
Talking in Whispers

Edith Wharton
Ethan Frome

William Wordsworth
Selected Poems

A Choice of Poets

Mystery Stories of the Nineteenth Century including The Signalman

Nineteenth Century Short Stories

Poetry of the First World War

Six Women Poets

For the AQA Anthology:
Duffy and Armitage & Pre-1914 Poetry

Heaney and Clarke & Pre-1914 Poetry

Poems from Different Cultures

Margaret Atwood
Cat's Eye
The Handmaid's Tale

Jane Austen
Emma
Mansfield Park
Persuasion
Pride and Prejudice
Sense and Sensibility

Alan Bennett
Talking Heads

William Blake
Songs of Innocence and of Experience

Charlotte Brontë
Jane Eyre
Villette

Emily Brontë
Wuthering Heights

Angela Carter
Nights at the Circus

Geoffrey Chaucer
The Franklin's Prologue and Tale
The Merchant's Prologue and Tale
The Miller's Prologue and Tale
The Prologue to the Canterbury Tales
The Wife of Bath's Prologue and Tale

Samuel Coleridge
Selected Poems

Joseph Conrad
Heart of Darkness

Daniel Defoe
Moll Flanders

Charles Dickens
Bleak House
Great Expectations
Hard Times

Emily Dickinson
Selected Poems

John Donne
Selected Poems

Carol Ann Duffy
Selected Poems

George Eliot
Middlemarch
The Mill on the Floss

T.S. Eliot
Selected Poems
The Waste Land

F. Scott Fitzgerald
The Great Gatsby

E.M. Forster
A Passage to India

Brian Friel
Translations

Thomas Hardy
Jude the Obscure
The Mayor of Casterbridge
The Return of the Native
Selected Poems
Tess of the d'Urbervilles

Seamus Heaney
Selected Poems from 'Opened Ground'

Nathaniel Hawthorne
The Scarlet Letter

Homer
The Iliad
The Odyssey

Aldous Huxley
Brave New World

Kazuo Ishiguro
The Remains of the Day

Ben Jonson
The Alchemist

James Joyce
Dubliners

John Keats
Selected Poems

Philip Larkin
The Whitsun Weddings and Selected Poems

Christopher Marlowe
Doctor Faustus
Edward II

Arthur Miller
Death of a Salesman

John Milton
Paradise Lost Books I & II

Toni Morrison
Beloved

George Orwell
Nineteen Eighty-Four

Sylvia Plath
Selected Poems

Alexander Pope
Rape of the Lock & Selected Poems

William Shakespeare
Antony and Cleopatra
As You Like It
Hamlet
Henry IV Part I
King Lear
Macbeth
Measure for Measure
The Merchant of Venice
A Midsummer Night's Dream
Much Ado About Nothing
Othello
Richard II
Richard III
Romeo and Juliet
The Taming of the Shrew
The Tempest
Twelfth Night
The Winter's Tale

George Bernard Shaw
Saint Joan

Mary Shelley
Frankenstein

Jonathan Swift
Gulliver's Travels and A Modest Proposal

Alfred Tennyson
Selected Poems

Virgil
The Aeneid

Alice Walker
The Color Purple

Oscar Wilde
The Importance of Being Earnest

Tennessee Williams
A Streetcar Named Desire
The Glass Menagerie

Jeanette Winterson
Oranges Are Not the Only Fruit

John Webster
The Duchess of Malfi

Virginia Woolf
To the Lighthouse

William Wordsworth
The Prelude and Selected Poems

W.B. Yeats
Selected Poems

Metaphysical Poets